Bodymapping

Kathy Illian

krause publications

700 East State Street, Iola, WI 54990-0001
www.krause.com

Please call or write for our free catalog of publications. Our toll-free number to place an order or obtain a free catalog is 800-258-0929 or please use our regular business telephone 715-445-2214 for editorial comment and further information.

The following registered trademark terms and companies appear in this publication:
Bodymapping™
Pendleton®
Vogue®
Butterick®
Burda®
Simplicity®
Style®
McCalls®
Band-Aid®

Photographs by Kathy Illian, unless otherwise noted
Illustrations by Eric Merrill
Book design by Jan Wojtech

Library of Congress Cataloging-In-Publication Data

Illian, Kathy
Bodymapping
1. sewing   2. pattern drafting   3. title

ISBN 0-87341-625-2
CIP 98-87278

Photograph on page 4 courtesy Amy Williams
Photograph on page 5 by Earl Gibson

DEDICATION

This book is dedicated to the five people who most inspired it:

Clem Conklin, my father, who gave me my analytical side.

Pat Conklin Cerf, my mother, who gave me my creative side.

Nancy Fullerton and Barbara Hunton, my vocational school sewing instructors, who introduced me to the world of fine sewing and pattern making.

The memory of Ernest Kumar, fine tailor, whose vast knowledge died with him far too soon.

ACKNOWLEDGMENTS

First and foremost, I must thank the many clients I've had over the years who unknowingly served as "guinea pigs" in my quest for fitting answers, especially Andrea Kelly, Mildred Del Guidice, Judy Lally, and Seeme Hasan.

I owe enormous thanks to the many people who have supported me and this project:

My models, many of whom also doubled as seamstresses, photographic assistants, caterers, baby sitters, and therapists, and who turned into some of the best friends a person could have: Ruby Forbes, Linda Olmsted, Andrea Kelly, Nettie Teuscher, Valarie Jenson, Jan McKinley, Ann Baxter-Stailey, Kathy Langan, Laurel Peterson, Jennifer Hebner, Darcy Nick, Lorie Roseff-Zapf, Cindi Grant, Stephanie Grant, Amy Williams, Mamie Healer, Bonnie Forrester, and Betty Johnston.

My neighbors, Paul and Linda Stowell, Steve and Cindi Grant, Jim and Tammy Peek, and Joe and Kate Snapp, for allowing me to use their beautiful homes for photo shoots.

My co-photographer, Earl Gibson, for his hard work and great ideas.

My editor, Amy Tincher-Durik, and the others I've worked with at Krause Publications, for making this a very stream-lined, painless, and fun process.

My colleagues at the Colorado Chapter of the Professional Association of Custom Clothiers, especially Mary Beth Davis, Kit Stanford, Jan McKinley, Mamie Healer, and Carol Kimball.

I'm especially grateful to my family and friends for their enthusiastic and unquestioning support:

My parents, Clem and Elizabeth Conklin and Pat and Ken Cerf, for everything, and because they're my friends as well as my parents.

My in-laws, Melvin and Joan Illian, for all their support throughout the years.

My sisters, Michelle Borton, Monica Conklin, and especially Darla Fears, for their love, help, and advice.

The rest of my immediate family, including Chris Conklin, Dennis and Diane Conklin, Hank Fears, my nephew Brandon, and my nieces Destiny, Angela, Sarah, Kayte, Kelsey, and Kari, for being a part of my wonderful clan.

My best friends, including Dave and Donna Bryant, Eric and Lorie Zapf, Landy and Caroline Alvarado and the whole Alvarado family, Helen Nichols, and Mady Nichols Todd, for their long-standing love and support.

Mostly, I thank the Almighty for the many gifts I enjoy and I thank my husband Larry and my beautiful daughters, Natalie and Lindsay, for all of their love.

TABLE OF CONTENTS

CHAPTER 1
What is Bodymapping?. **5**

CHAPTER 2
Draping the Bodymap. **16**

CHAPTER 3
Making a Base Pattern **36**

CHAPTER 4
Pattern Drafting: Tops,
Jackets, and Dresses. **64**

APPENDIX 1
Dart Angle Comparison **114**

APPENDIX 2
Making Asymmetry
Adjustments **116**

APPENDIX 3
Borrowing Collars,
Necklines, and Closures
from Commercial Patterns. . . . **116**

INDEX **120**

CHAPTER 1

WHAT IS BODYMAPPING?

Ask any sewing enthusiast what the hardest part of sewing clothes is, and they'll probably say "fitting." Why is fitting so hard? There are several reasons, and they all have to do with the relationship between commercial sewing patterns and the sewers who use them. First of all, most people require that a pattern be changed or altered in order to fit them properly. Why? Because human bodies exist in such infinite variety. Therefore, the combination of pattern alterations each individual requires is as unique as the body's own DNA. Commercial sewing patterns are usually designed for just one symmetrical body type, one posture, one height, and one proportion, and in the case of women, one bra cup size. Even if we are close to the "ideal" body type at one point in time, as a teenager perhaps, eventually our bodies change—and they keep changing over the years for many reasons, including childbirth, illness, weight gain or loss, and athletic activity. Our lifestyles have a profound effect on our physical state: our posture becomes more round-shouldered if we spend a lot of time at a desk or workbench, and more erect if we have a military or dance background. Propping a toddler on a hip or carrying a heavy shoulder bag can affect the symmetry of our bodies. Our proportions change through the years as well, as muscle is slowly replaced by fat. All of these changes affect the fit of our clothing. Even without weight change, what fits us perfectly at age 25 may not be even close when we reach 45. Consequently, most garment makers must perform pattern alterations on each and every pattern they use.

But pattern alteration is confusing to many sewers, primarily because the experts teach fitting and pattern alteration using a "fitting shell" or "sloper"—a basic pattern from which fashion patterns are derived (Fig. 1-1). The fitting shell includes a bodice and skirt that are divided by a waistline seam, and this fundamentally horizontal waistline seam is adjusted for most individuals—as in the case of a large (or small) bust or abdomen, full or flat buttocks, swayback, or uneven hips, to name a few. But a glance into any current pattern catalogue will show that we don't wear many garments with waistline seams anymore. Long gone are the dresses that actually resemble the fitting shell pattern. Instead we see separates like tunics, hip-length or longer jackets, blouses, and sweatshirts over pants, skirts, and leggings. These are the clothes we wear now: tops that extend past the waist. This crucial fitting line has vanished, leaving us with one less tool to achieve perfect fit.

How do we change patterns that look completely different from the fitting shell? For example, how do we add extra length for the bust, abdomen, or buttocks for a dress or long jacket when we've been taught to do it at the waist? All too often, we simply make the relevant length change at the hem, which results in a bias and hard-to-handle hem line, and more importantly, in a cross grain line which strains and pulls the fabric up and away from the body as it tries to hang horizontally. This is but a Band-Aid for an imperfect garment.

Even if we've succeeded in perfecting the fitting shell pattern, we may not know how to change more contemporary patterns, because we don't really understand how they relate to the fitting shell. And most individual bodies require combination alterations—one change affects one part of the pattern, which affects another part, and so on. Additionally, commercial patterns vary greatly in the amount of design ease, or looseness, in each garment, so even though the sketch or photo indicates a certain fit, the actual pattern may have much more or less ease. To further complicate matters, the various pattern companies use different specifications for their basic fitting patterns, so sewers must perfect a fitting shell made by each individual pattern company. It's no wonder so many give up on garment-making.

There's a fundamental flaw in the "pattern alteration" method of fitting instruction: sewers have

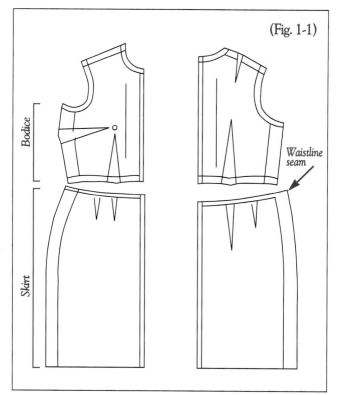

The basic fitting shell

(Fig. 1-1)

Bodice

Skirt

Waistline seam

never been taught what proper fitting really is. Pattern alteration is not fitting. It is the procedure used to change a pattern after the fitting question has been answered. Fitting is the act of determining the proper size and shape of a garment that will conform to an individual body.

There is an obvious need for an easier and more exact approach to understanding fitting. This book details a streamlined fitting process called Bodymapping, which results in a perfectly-fitted base garment with no waistline seam, and is done without measuring the body. Although the measuring tape is one of the most important sewing tools we have, it can be imprecise in fitting because it only reveals a small part of the whole at a time, and it relies heavily on the fitter's *opinion* for its placement on the body. The measuring tape tends to follow the contours of the body—the hills and valleys—more than a garment, which hangs from the shoulders and skims the curves of the body in a straighter manner. These factors lead to discrepancies at the very start of the fitting process.

Bodymapping uses the body as its template, much as a carpenter traces around the old piece of wood to make an outline for its replacement. The Bodymap pattern is accomplished by draping a poncho-like length of gingham on the body, pinning out excess fabric where needed, and marking on it the body's landmarks—the crucial reference points that must be in their proper positions for perfect fit. Bodymapping doesn't require that you have prior sewing or fitting experience. In fact, it's as easy as wrapping a present. You don't use your measuring tape to wrap a box; you simply lay the box on the wrapping paper, cut enough paper to go around, and then fold in the extra paper at the corners. In Bodymapping, the body is the box, gingham is the wrapping paper, and the curves of the body are the corners.

There's little room for error in performing the Bodymapping process: the gingham's bold squares make it obvious when a grain line is wrong, and the bust points, waistline, armholes, and shoulder blades are marked right onto the fabric, creating a blueprint of the body. Correctly done, it results in a perfectly-balanced garment, with the cross grain line of the fabric parallel to the floor at the chest, upper back, hip, and hem line. You can easily double-check that it's been done properly by measuring from the floor to a horizontal line on each side of the body—they should measure the same. You'll see the real value in Bodymapping after you've pinned the shoulder area (the very first step in the process) because you've just eliminated the necessity of having to alter for as many as twelve different "flaws," including square or sloped shoulders, high or shallow neck base, large or thin neck, broad or narrow shoulders, forward neck, and forward arm joints.

After executing the Bodymapping process, you will convert the fabric Bodymap into a Bodymap base pattern—your personal sloper. You'll use a pen to mark the placement of the pins before removing them, lay the gingham out in a single layer on a table, and cover it with tracing paper. Then you'll simply trace over all your pin and placement marks. At this point you have a rough map of the body, which is far superior to a list of measurements. Every measurement you could ever need or want is right there on the Bodymap—an incredible advantage if you happen to be sewing for an out-of-towner, or when you don't have the actual body there to re-check. Step-by-step instructions are given for you to refine and "true" the markings. This means you'll use a straightedge and a French curve to ensure that you've achieved accurate seam lines and smooth transitions between parts of the pattern that are supposed to fit together. You'll learn how to put darts in their proper position and how much ease is needed in certain areas, such as the armhole, for proper fit and comfort.

Once a basic pattern has been perfected "grain-wise," any garment derived from it will be grain-perfect too. Because there is no waistline seam, like most of the clothes we wear today, the Bodymap base pattern is slightly less fitted at the waist than a standard fitting shell, and can be used to design just about any top pattern you'd see in a commercial pattern catalogue, once you learn the pattern drafting techniques covered in this book. You will learn how to incorporate your sloper into fifteen basic blocks, or master patterns, which can be used "as is" or as the basis for more complex fashion patterns.

Additionally, you'll learn the precise steps needed to "superimpose" commercial patterns over your perfectly-fitted variation patterns, so that you are gaining the details that attracted you to the pattern in the first place. After an investment of only a few hours on an afternoon or two, you'll be able to use your Bodymap patterns in conjunction with commercial patterns—without having the headaches of testing the fit again and again.

In addition to designing your own perfectly-fitted fashion patterns, you'll gain a much fuller understanding of exactly how real bodies differ from the standardized measurements used in basic pattern making, whether the pattern ends up as a commercial sewing pattern or as a store-bought garment. Many sewers have grown up thinking the most important part of fitting concerns the measurement around the bust, waist, and hips. In fact, these are the easy measurements to work with—just make sure you have enough to go around! Taking in or letting out a side seam is elementary compared to the intricate finessing of the upper part of a pattern that is required as a result of bust projection, posture, and stance. You'll learn that there are sometimes compromises to be made in pattern making, that there are limitations in the ways you can balance the look, the fit, and the comfort of a particular garment.

There are many aspects of proper fitting that are commonly misunderstood, but seven of them stand out as the ones which seem to cause the most problems. I'll introduce these elements to you now briefly, but you'll really start to comprehend them after reading about and performing the Bodymapping process. These elements include fitting by grain, attaining proper garment balance, correcting neck size, managing width imbalance from top to bottom, understanding the sleeve/armhole connection, identifying the limitations in waist suppression found in garments which extend past the waist, and applying garment contouring.

FITTING BY GRAIN

This element is the core around which Bodymapping is centered. What exactly is fitting by grain? In order to understand this concept, you must first familiarize yourself with certain terms related to fabric and garments (See also Fig. 1-2):

Lengthwise grain line, also called "straight of grain," or "straight grain line." When fabric is woven on a loom, the threads are arranged in two directions, vertical and horizontal. The vertical, or warp threads, are stretched taut on the loom first, then the horizontal, or weft threads, are woven under and over the warp threads at a 90° angle to them. Thus the vertical, or lengthwise, grain of the fabric is the direction with the least amount of stretch, or give. Lengthwise grain is called the strongest grain, and the length of a fabric piece is the measurement of the lengthwise edge (called the selvage).

NOTE: Woven fabrics are the focus of this book. Knit fabrics, which are comprised of one intertwining thread or yarn, are quite forgiving in fitting because of the fabric's ability to stretch and mold to the body. Once you perfect the fit with a woven fabric, you'll learn to adapt your patterns to knits in the pattern drafting chapter.

Crosswise grain line, also called "cross grain line." The horizontal, or crosswise, threads stretch a little more because of the extra length gained as the threads move over and under the warp threads. Crosswise grain is not as strong as the lengthwise grain. The width of a fabric piece is the measurement across the crosswise edge which, for garment making,

usually falls between 36 and 60 inches wide, with the majority of fabrics being 45 inches wide.

Bias grain line. Bias is any grain line on the fabric that is neither lengthwise nor crosswise. A true bias is exactly 45° from both the lengthwise and the crosswise grain, and is easily found by folding the fabric so that a lengthwise thread falls on top of a crosswise thread. The fold line is the true bias. True bias is the stretchiest, and therefore the weakest, grain line. Additionally, there are two directions for true bias on each piece of cloth, which often hang or "fall" differently, one side stretching more than the other.

Grain up. This means you identify both the lengthwise and the crosswise grains of the fabric and determine whether they are at an exact 90° angle to each other. Find the crosswise grain by cutting into the selvage of the fabric, about an inch from the end, and tear it across the crosswise direction. If it won't tear, pull a crosswise thread and cut across on the resulting puckered line to the other side. Fold the fabric in half along the lengthwise grain. If the selvages and crosswise edges lay right on top of each other, and the fabric is completely flat with no ripples, the fabric is grained up, or "on-grain." If not, the fabric is "off-grain" and must be straightened.

Straighten the grain. Pull the shorter fabric corner along the true bias until it lengthens to equal the longer side (Fig. 1-3). Sometimes you can do this with an iron or with slightly dampened fabric, and sometimes it just can't be straightened. If you can't straighten it, ignore the crosswise grain and cut the edge at right angles to the selvage. (This technique of ignoring the crosswise grain is only effective in fabric used for test garments or in firmly-woven fabrics with little drape. Ideally, you should only use on-grain fabrics for your garment-making.)

Dart. Darts are triangular sections of fabric which are

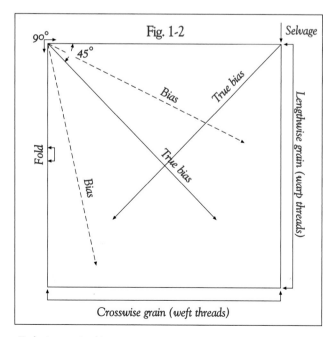

Fabric grain lines

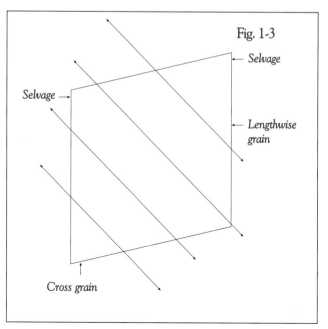

Pull the fabric along the true bias until the lengthwise and crosswise grain lines are at 90-degree angles.

folded out in order to provide shape for the curves of the body. (For the anatomy of a dart, see Fig. 1-4.) The amount of fabric pinned out in the dart is called dart "take-up" or "underlay." In this respect, dart take-up can be compared to the sections of paper folded under at the corners of a box when wrapping a present. Although darts are clearly recognizable when marked as "sewn darts," they can be "manipulated" by the pattern designer, which means they can be moved to different locations, converted into gathers, pleats, ease, or style lines, or simply released to form a less fitted garment. These transformations can make it hard for sewers to understand where the shaping is in a pattern. In a base pattern used for pattern drafting, darts extend all the way to the center of the curve (called a pivot point) for which they are providing shape. For example, in a sloper, the bust dart is drawn right to the bust point, whereas in a garment, the bust dart stops short about an inch or so away. This is because the curves of the body are rounded, not pointed, and by stopping short, extra fabric remains to accommodate the fullness of the body curve. A dart is moved by pivoting its legs to another location, and even though it may appear to have changed in size when moved from, for example, the side seam to the shoulder seam, in fact the angle of the dart remains constant; only the amount of dart take-up at the originating seam has changed (Fig. 1-5). This means that from the bust point to an arbitrary point, say, 3 inches away, the angle of the dart (and therefore the dart size) is the same no matter where the dart starts from. In Bodymapping, this angle is referred to as the "bust dart angle," meaning the angle of the dart in a base pattern at 3 inches away from the bust point. The difference between a commercial pattern's inherent bust dart angle and the subject's own bust dart angle is a crucial comparison for proper pattern alteration.

In perfect fitting, the ideal is to achieve a lengthwise grain that falls vertically down the body, and a crosswise grain that hangs horizontally across the body, parallel to the floor at the chest, upper back, hip, and hem line. The lengthwise grain is controlled by gravity, and the crosswise grain is controlled by pinning out darts where the curves or bumps of the body occur. The control of the cross grain line, or "fitting by grain," is the essence of Bodymapping. This no-sew, from-the-top-down process eliminates the need for cutting, slashing, spreading, repositioning the bust dart, and other time-consuming "alterations" usually performed before testing a fitting shell, and fitting the body is reduced to one scientific fact: gravity controls grain.

NOTE: Some garments have the bias grain line substituted for the straight grain, which creates a fluid and drapey garment. These designs require a reasonably high skill level to sew perfectly. Bodymapping concentrates on straight-grained garment making, although once perfected, some Bodymap patterns can be used with the bias grain substituted for the straight.

The following points will demonstrate how grain works in conjunction with your garment:

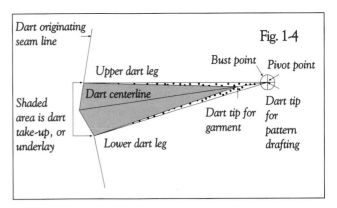

Fig. 1-4

The anatomy of a dart

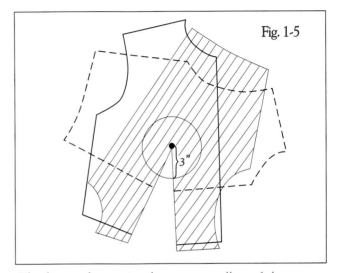

Fig. 1-5

The dart angle remains the same regardless of the distance to the originating seam line.

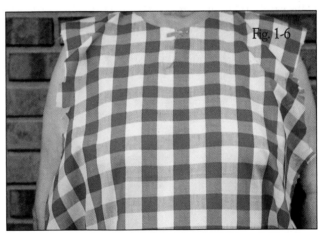

Fig. 1-6

In the front, the garment initially balances on the neck points.

❶ Bodies are asymmetrical in many ways, which means that the right and left sides of the body may require different sized darts to correctly control the cross grain line.

❷ In front, the garment initially balances on the neck points (Fig. 1-6). On a symmetrically-shouldered body, the cross grain line of the garment is parallel to the floor between the neck points and above the bust. On a body with a lowered shoulder, the neck point is usually also lower, and would require additional fabric pinned out (in other words, more "take-up") in order to keep the cross grain line horizontal.

❸ The shoulder slope dart then takes over control of the garment from the neck points to the shoulder points, above the bust (Fig. 1-7). Again, a lowered shoulder point would require more take-up than the higher one.

❹ The bust dart controls the cross grain of the garment from the bust point to the side of the garment, and ultimately controls the change in length from the center of the garment to the side (Fig. 1-8A and B).

❺ In the back, the garment initially balances on the back neck and neck points, except in the case of a dowager's hump, where the garment initially balances mainly on the center back neck point. The shoulder slope dart then takes over control of the grain of the garment from the neck to the shoulder point above the shoulder blade.

❻ The upper back dart controls the cross grain of the garment from the shoulder blade to the side of the body, usually to a much lesser extent than the bust dart does in the front, because it is normally smaller.

❼ The waist darts simply taper the garment in at the waist, nothing more (Fig. 1-9). Consequently, waist shaping is easily fine-tuned at a fitting.

Therefore, for perfect fit, the integrity of all grain-controlling darts must be maintained. For most women, the bust darts have the largest impact on the grain lines of the garment, followed closely by the shoulder slope darts. The upper back darts become larger and more important as the upper back rounds, but in most cases are smaller than the bust darts. Because most patterns are designed for a "B" cup, women with larger cup sizes (and therefore larger bust dart angles) have a much harder time fitting into commercial patterns, particu-

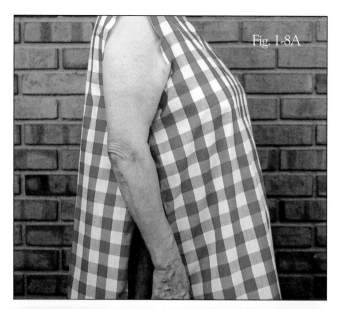

Fig. 1-8A

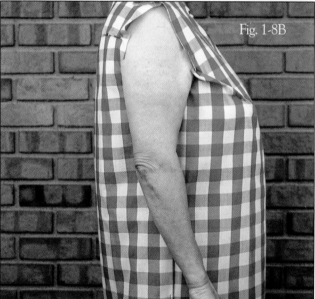

Fig. 1-8B

The bust dart controls the grain of the garment from the bust point to the side of the garment and it ultimately controls the change in length from the center of the garment to the side.

Fig. 1-7

The shoulder slope dart then takes over control of the grain of the garment from the neck point to the shoulder point above the bust.

The waist dart simply tapers the garment in at the waist, nothing more.

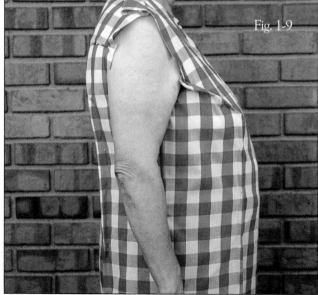

Fig. 1-9

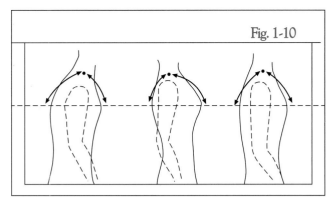

Fig. 1-10

Although these figures may have the same bust measurement, and therefore would take the same sized pattern, they would each need quite different alterations in order to attain the proper garment balance.

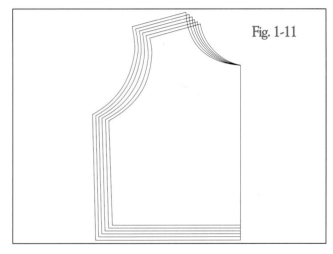

Fig. 1-11

Commercial patterns are graded, which means that the overall pattern increases from size to size according to a standard grading chart.

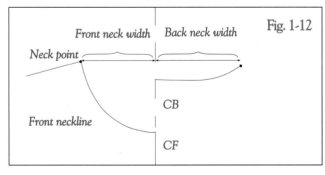

Fig. 1-12

Neck width is the horizontal distance from the neck point to the center of the garment.

larly those where the bust shaping has been reduced or eliminated.

ATTAINING PROPER GARMENT BALANCE

Proper balance of a garment is probably the most important requirement for comfort in a garment. Proper balance is achieved by having the correct length from the neck point to the bust line, both in front and back. (The neck point is the highest point of the shoulder, at the neck's base, and the bust line is an imaginary line on a garment that's parallel to the floor at bust point level). The average commercial pattern has a slightly longer front length than back length, because the average bust protrudes more than the average shoulder blade, but of course this is not always the case. The following illustration exemplifies the differences among these subjects with the same bust measurement and cup size, who presumably would take the same sized pattern (Fig. 1-10).

As you can see, they are a study in contrasts. The pattern would have to be changed individually for every one of them, and in more than one way. Each person has a unique combination of physical factors that affects the balance and comfort of a garment, and to ignore these factors means to be uncomfortable in a garment that keeps falling to the back, to the front, or from side to side.

CORRECTING NECK SIZE

Appropriate neck size has a direct bearing on the comfort of the garment as well and is another source of frustration for sewers. The fit of the neck points and the proper alignment of the shoulder seam rely on a neckline that is neither too narrow nor too wide. In the commercial pattern industry, as well as in garment manufacturing, patterns are "graded," which means that the overall pattern increases proportionally from size to size, according to a standard grading chart (Fig. 1-11). However, as you know, real bodies don't necessarily increase in proportion to standard measurements—the neck and shoulders don't necessarily get wider just because the bust gets bigger! Because the neck widths (the horizontal distance from the neck point to the center of the garment) on commercial patterns increase incrementally as the pattern bust size increases, many pattern neck widths are much wider than the individual's personal neck width—especially for larger-busted women who have chosen their pattern according to their bust size (Fig. 1-12). Additionally, the neck widths of the back and front are often unequal on real bodies— usually the back neck is wider. As youthful straight posture gives way to a more forward-shouldered stance, the back neck widens. (Place a fingertip on your neck point and slowly move your shoulders forward, as if hunching over. Your neck hasn't gotten bigger, the back neckline has simply widened.) You probably require a wider back neck width (and therefore, a narrower front neck width) if pinching fabric all the way down center front (CF) makes the shoulders and neckline fit you better. This technique, when used in pattern drafting, widens the entire back of the garment in the appropriate place. Conversely, an over-erect posture would require an equal or narrower back neck width than front neck width. On a garment pattern, the back neckline is narrowed or widened by moving the center back in or out *horizontally*, not by moving the neck points up or down—the center back neck position is usually 3/4 inch below the level of the neck points, although it can vary between 1/2 and 1 inch below (Fig. 1-13). The front neckline *depth* is more variable than the back's and is easily marked at a fitting when the neck points are in the right place.

MANAGING WIDTH IMBALANCE FROM TOP TO BOTTOM

Another confusing aspect of proper fitting concerns the subject who has a much larger top than bottom, or vice versa. Examples of this body type would include a very large-busted woman with small hips, a small-busted woman with very large hips, thighs, or protruding abdomen, someone with extremely protruding buttocks, or possibly a woman with a severely rounded back that protrudes well past the buttocks in profile. These are some of the subjects who will require more fitting seams than just the bust, upper back, and waist darts we see in a garment that extends past the waist, in order for the cross grain at the hem line to remain parallel to the floor. Must they have a waistline seam to accommodate this difference from top to bottom? No, but they must have either a horizontal seam somewhere between the bust and hip line, or an extra vertical seam on each side of the body (a princess line seam) in order to narrow or widen the fabric needed as the garment hangs from top to bottom. Because Bodymapping concentrates on garments without a horizontal fitting line, these subjects will be instructed on how to incorporate their Bodymap into a base princess line pattern.

UNDERSTANDING THE SLEEVE/ARMHOLE CONNECTION

The next element involves the set-in sleeve and its relationship to the armhole. Why is it so hard to set in a tailored sleeve without wrinkles or diagonal folds? Why do so many jacket patterns have such wide shoulders? Why are pattern armholes so big? These are just a few of the multitude of questions sewers have about sleeves. Again, the answers lie in assessing the differences between the armholes and arms of real bodies versus those on which the commercial patterns are based. Understanding how the parts of sleeves are drafted in the first place explains a lot about the sleeve/armhole relationship (Fig. 1-14).

In order for a set-in sleeve to fall correctly, there must be an ample amount of fabric from the neck point, over the shoul-

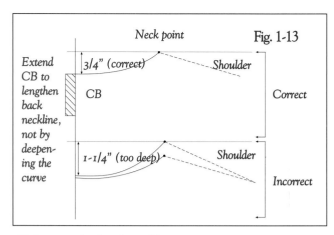

Fig. 1-13

Widening the back neckline

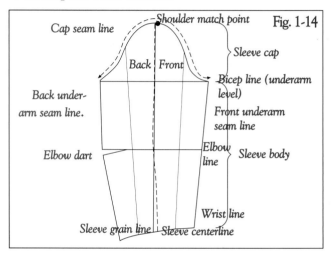

Fig. 1-14

The parts of a sleeve

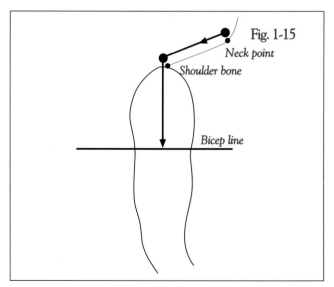

Fig. 1-15

In order for a set-in sleeve to fall correctly, there must be an ample amount of fabric from the neck point, over the shoulder bone to the bicep (under-arm level) line.

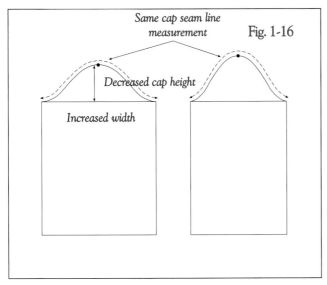

Fig. 1-16

Same cap seam line measurement

Decreased cap height

Increased width

These sleeves will fit into the same armhole.

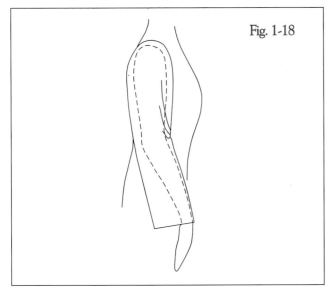

Fig. 1-17

Leave open

Leave open

CF

CB

The armholes on many commercial patterns are enlarged by the manipulation of bust and upper back darts; the darts are moved into the armhole and left open as ease.

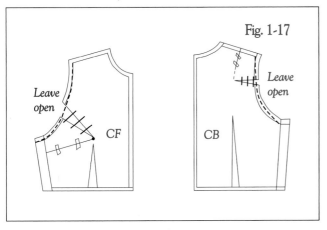

Fig. 1-18

The arm hangs vertically from the shoulder to the elbow, where it curves gently forward. This forward bend causes diagonal folds to form on the front of the sleeve.

der bone, to the bicep (underarm level) line (Fig. 1-15).

The shoulder seam supplies part of this length, and then the sleeve "cap," or the part of the sleeve above the bicep line, takes over. Too little length supplied by the shoulder seam results in a sleeve that catches on the fleshy part of the upper arm, which is why the arm fullness must be considered more heavily than the position of the actual shoulder bone when determining a length for the shoulder seam. If there's too little length in either the shoulder seam or the sleeve cap, the resulting sleeves have diagonal folds in the upper portion. Rather than hanging perfectly as the arms rest at the sides of the body, they only fall smoothly when the arms are held out at an angle from the body. Why would a pattern be designed with insufficient cap height? Because in order to provide as wide and comfortable a sleeve as possible, the pattern designer must sometimes make compromises—when the bicep width (the widest part of the basic sleeve, at the underarm level) increases, the cap height (the part of the sleeve that lies above the bicep width) decreases, and vice versa, in order to fit into the same armhole (Fig. 1-16).

So, when the bicep width is increased, the cap height must be reduced and, therefore, the required length from the neck point can *only* be made up by lengthening the shoulder seam, resulting in a wider shoulder span. But who wants wider shoulders than the patterns already offer? Most women lament the broad-shouldered look of many commercial patterns, and many automatically shorten the shoulder seam length, perhaps without realizing the consequences.

Furthermore, the armholes on many commercial fashion patterns are enlarged by the manipulation of bust and upper back darts. That is, the darts are moved into the armhole and left open as ease (Fig. 1-17). This change provides a larger armhole, which in turn requires a larger sleeve, and because the distance from shoulder point to underarm point increases with the extra length in the armhole, the requirement for cap height increases as well, compounding the problem.

The lower part of the arm is also an important factor in fitting the sleeve. The arm normally hangs vertically from the shoulder to the elbow, where it curves gently forward. This forward bend causes the arm to strike the front of the sleeve, which in turn causes diagonal folds to appear on the front part of the sleeve (Fig. 1-18). This effect is emphasized on those with a more pronounced arm curve, often found on those who work with their hands constantly bent forward at the elbows, such as typists, machinists, and dressmakers. Usually, sewers are instructed to try on the sleeve and shift some of the front cap towards the back if this occurs, tilting the cross grain line of the sleeve in the process. Part of the Bodymapping process includes the proper analyzation of the armhole and arm curve and instructions on how to draft a sleeve which will fall perfectly. You'll also see why a two-part sleeve is the best choice for those arms which curve a little more than average. Bodymapping focuses on achieving the optimum shoulder/sleeve/armhole relationship in a truly custom way. The subject is given the information she needs to evaluate which of the three interrelated factors are the most important to her: shoulder seam length, sleeve width, or the perfect fall of the sleeve when the arm is at rest.

IDENTIFYING LIMITATIONS IN WAIST SUPPRESSION

In order to understand why many garments develop diagonal folds when the waist side seams are taken in, you must remember a basic principle of mathematics: the shortest distance between two points is a straight line. Fig. 1-19 demonstrates how this principle is applied to waist shaping in garments.

As you can see, the side seam length gets longer as it becomes more diagonal, and when trued (side seams matched up as they'll be sewn and blended with a French curve), the side seam requires more and more length the closer to the garment center it gets. The problem is, in a one-piece garment with no waistline seam, there is no extra length available, other than the amount the fabric might stretch as it moves closer to true bias. The waist can only be taken in to the extent that the hip cross grain line remains level. Consequently, over-shaping the side seams results in diagonal folds from the bust to the side waist in the front, and from the shoulder blade to the side waist in back, a problem which increases as the difference between the waist and the bust and/or hips increases. A protruding bust would also require more length to tightly fit the waist, length that is not available on garments with no waistline seam (Fig. 1-20). The solution is to apply the waist suppression in as many places as possible: the center back, in some cases the center front, the four waist darts (one on either side of center front and center back) which can each be divided into two or three smaller darts, and the side seams. This way the length increase is minimal, but the waist suppression is handled smoothly and without unsightly folds. It's also important to note that it can be very unflattering to take in the waist so much, even if it's done correctly, that it over-emphasizes certain figure flaws, as in the case of a person with both a tiny waist and very full thighs. In conclusion, the waist suppression in a particular garment must be "relative" to the design, the fabric, and the body type.

APPLYING GARMENT CONTOURING

As mentioned previously, a garment that hangs from the shoulders tends to skim over the curves of the body (Fig. 1-21). However, any time you lower or widen a neckline substantially from the basic round, or jewel, neck, or change a sleeved garment into a sleeveless one, the contours of the actual shoulders, armhole, and chest area must be compensated for or gaping will probably occur in these areas. The amount of contouring depends on the actual body and the chosen design—a basic tank top will need just a little contour-

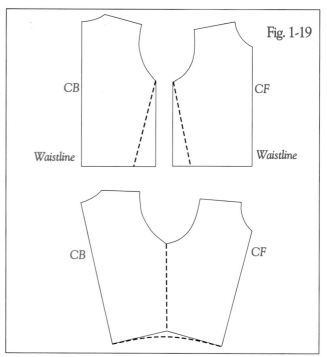

The length of the side seam increases when it becomes more diagonal (top). When trued, the side seam requires even more length. This extra length is not available with garments with no waistline seam (bottom).

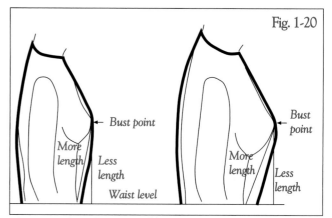

A protruding bust would require more length to tightly fit the waist, length that is not available on garments with no waistline seam.

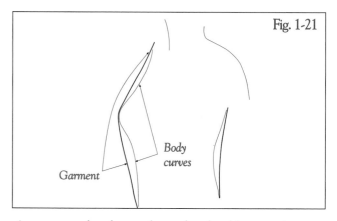

A garment that hangs from the shoulders tends to skim over the curves of the body in a straight manner.

Fig. 1-22

Check for additional contouring needs at a muslin fitting.

ing, while a strapless dress will need quite a lot. Contouring the front pattern is performed by cutting the pattern to the bust point from an outside seam line (i.e., the armhole, the shoulder seam, the neckline, or center front (CF)) and overlapping this cut while spreading apart the existing bust dart. Because this technique results in a larger bust dart that may become too large for the shape it is meant to fit, converting darted patterns to princess line patterns is often advisable, depending on the amount of contouring to be done, because princess lines can always be blended at the bust point if the shaping becomes too pointed, whereas darts cannot be. All contoured patterns should be tested in muslin and fine-tuned before cutting into a more expensive fabric (Fig. 1-22).

Once you understand how important it is to control the fitting elements mentioned above, you'll begin to revise your relationship with commercial sewing patterns. You'll start to realize that patterns are intended merely as a starting point for garment sewers. Commercial pattern companies hire talented designers to transform cutting-edge fashion into pattern form, thus providing home sewers with access to designer clothing at a fraction of the cost. There's really no way pattern companies could ever make one pattern fit every single person perfectly, but they could give us much more detailed information on how to use their patterns effectively, primarily by educating us on how their patterns are drafted—how they're changed from the basic fitting shell to fashion patterns which look nothing like it. By not doing so, they've really done themselves (and us) a disservice, because the majority of us don't understand how to change them in order to make them fit. The challenge now is to provide pattern users with the information they need to take this "pattern-as-starting-point" and turn it into a garment that fits and is comfortable.

Bodymapping fills this educational void by first showing how to perfect a base pattern using an easy, measureless technique, and then explaining how patterns are made and changed into the garments we wear. After completing your Bodymap pattern, which takes me about an hour from start to finish, you may use the information you've learned to as little or as great an extent as you like. For instance, you may simply analyze some of its measurements in order to fine-tune a blouse pattern you're having trouble with, or you may decide to draft all of your set-in sleeves with the instructions you'll find in Chapter 3. But hopefully, you'll take the time to draft a few custom patterns for yourself, for it is in learning about pattern drafting that the secrets of fitting are finally understood. The Bodymapping process converts the "art" of fitting into the "science" of fitting.

CHAPTER 2
DRAPING THE BODYMAP

Before you get started, you'll need to gather your supplies and prepare both the gingham and your subject for Bodymapping.

FAIRGATE

The basic supplies needed for Bodymapping

Optional supplies

SUPPLIES NEEDED FOR BODYMAPPING

❀ A HELPER

❀ 2 YARDS OF GINGHAM (YELLOW, BLUE, PINK, OR RED, ONE INCH GRID PREFERRED). Gingham, a woven two-color cloth with evenly-spaced checks of various sizes, is the fabric of choice for the Bodymapping process for the following reasons:

1) The bold checks make the grain lines very easy to read

2) Gingham is usually easy to grain up if found to be off-grain. Try to buy from a full bolt, because it's more likely to be on grain on the outside rather than on the inside.

The lighter colors are specified because it's hard to see your markings on the darker ones. If gingham is not available, use muslin. Muslin is an inexpensive fabric which is often off-grain. If it is, it will need to be straightened and marked with grain lines in order to use it for Bodymapping. Sometimes, the grain line of a fabric simply cannot be straightened perfectly. In this case, use the selvage as the lengthwise grain and draw in cross grain lines at right angles to the selvage (instructions follow).

Caution: Using off-grain fabric may result in less than perfect results. Use non-woven pattern cloth as a last resort, because there is no "give" on the bias and therefore the waist shaping is quite limited.

❀ NARROW TAPE (1/4 INCH MAXIMUM). The tape is used to delineate the sides of the body, as well as the natural shoulder line. If you must use a wider tape, cut it in half, lengthwise.

❀ NARROW ELASTIC (1/4 TO 1/2 INCH WIDE). This will be used to delineate the waistline, so measure off an amount that can be comfortably tied around the subject's waist.

❀ HALF-INCH THICK SET-IN SHOULDER PAD. Substitute a thicker pad if the subject desires.

❀ STICK-ON DOTS. Stick-on dots (color coding labels) are used as reference points.

❀ GENERAL SEWING SUPPLIES. Scissors (both fabric cutting and paper cutting), pins, marking pens, tape, and measuring tape.

❀ ONE YARD OF WEIGHTED ROPE OR NECKLACE WITH PENDANT. Weighted rope can be found in the drapery departments of many sewing stores. It's about 1/4 inch wide and is used to delineate the neckline. Use a necklace with a pendant or other weight attached to the bottom as an alternative. It should be at least 30 inches long, so that it hangs below the bust level.

❀ MEASURING AND DRAFTING TOOLS. Yardstick, straightedge, French or skirt curve, L-square, and compass.

❀ TRACING PAPER. Any kind of blank, transparent paper will do. Office and art supply stores generally offer a lightweight architect's or drafting paper that comes in various widths, but 30-inch paper is preferred.

❀ WORKING SURFACE. A flat table on which to lay out your Bodymap and your tracing paper.

❀ PROPER UNDERGARMENTS. It is essential that the subject wear the undergarments during Bodymapping that they plan to wear in the garments produced from the Bodymap. This primarily concerns bras and tummy control apparel like girdles and hip smoothers, which can move flesh into different areas.

❀ LEOTARD OR SLIP. As long as the leotard is fairly loose-fitting and doesn't bind any part of the body, it's very helpful in Bodymapping because it provides a surface on which to temporarily pin the gingham while smoothing it out to the sides. You could substitute a full slip or rib-knit tank top, but don't use anything with sleeves or something that's either too loose or tight fitting.

OPTIONAL BUT VERY HELPFUL SUPPLIES

❀ REMOVABLE TAPE. Removable tape is used any time you want to temporarily secure your pattern to the table or to another pattern piece, as in the truing process.

❀ FLEXIBLE RULER. An invaluable drafting tool for measuring curved lines, this ruler is available at office and drafting supply stores.

❀ CALCULATOR. If your math is rusty, this may come in handy. Listed below you'll find eighths converted to decimals:

1/8 = .125	1/4 = .25
3/8 = .375	1/2 = .5
5/8 = .625	3/4 = .75
7/8 = .875	

❀ GRIDDED PAPER. This is heavier than tracing paper and is marked with 1-inch grids that simplify the pattern drafting process. For the first draft of the Bodymap, I use regular tracing paper; then after I've manipulated the darts into differ-ent variation patterns, I transfer them to the heavier gridded paper. Sleeves are drafted onto the gridded paper. I strongly recommend the use of this paper for all of your pattern drafting for the simple reason that perpendicular lines are truly perpendicular, which is an intrinsic requirement for pattern drafting. You may use non-woven gridded pattern cloth, but it can sometimes stretch when moistened, which can distort the patterns.

❀ ADDING MACHINE TAPE. This is great for patching your patterns; it's often the right size to patch a dart under-lay.

❀ OAKTAG MANILA FILE FOLDER PAPER. It comes in large sheets or on rolls and is the final medium for patterns you'll use repeatedly. It is available through art supply stores.

❀ MARKING PENS, VARIOUS COLORS. Using different colors makes the truing process easier.

BODYMAPPING AT A GLANCE

1. Determine overall size of fabric poncho and trim away excess gingham.
2. Check grain of gingham and straighten if necessary.
3. Place weighted rope around subject's neck, measure, and record front neck width.
4. Trace appropriate neckline onto gingham's center and cut it out, adding slit at CF.
5. Trim away the armhole excess.
6. Tape the subject's shoulder lines and side seams and place stick-on dots at CB neck, neck points, and shoulder tip.
7. Place narrow elastic around the subject's waist.
8. Place the poncho on the subject and tape gingham in place at CB neck.
9. Tape the CF closed.
10. Pin the shoulder slope darts.
11. Pin the bust darts and mark the bust points, front draping points, and the bust radius.
12. Mark the shoulder blade points and pin the upper back darts.
13. Pin the side seams.
14. Trim armhole area, side seams, and hem line as needed.
15. Pin out the waist darts and mark the position of the waist elastic.
16. Mark position of underarm level onto gingham.
17. Mark same position with tape on arm.
18. Mark neck points onto weighted rope.
19. Check that shoulder pins end on top of taped shoulder line and adjust if necessary.
20. Measure and record any distance between weighted rope and marked CB neck point.
21. Mark position of the front neck level.
22. Determine and record back neck length, garment shoulder seam length, and cap height.
23. Measure bicep circumference.
24. Delineate wrist line and measure front and back arm lengths and elbow depth.
25. Mark positions of all pins.
26. Remove gingham, tape, elastic, and stick-on dots and record measurements on Pattern Drafting Personal Measurement Chart.

PREPARING TO BODYMAP

DETERMINE THE OVERALL SIZE OF THE FABRIC PONCHO

First, determine whether your gingham is on grain. If it's not, either straighten it, buy another piece, or use muslin which is marked with cross grain lines every 4 inches.* Next, trim some of the gingham's width away if it's not needed. To do this, with the selvages vertical, wrap a single length of gingham around the body so that the cross grain line extends smoothly from behind the underarm, around the front, and to the back of the other underarm (Fig. 2-1). Make a mark at this point and trim off any remaining fabric, straight down the grain. Cut, rather than tear, the excess because tearing seems to distort the fabric edge on gingham more than some other fabrics.

Next, fold the gingham in fourths by first folding it in half along a crosswise grain line, then again in half down a lengthwise grain. With a marking pen, place a dot at the folded tip, marking the center of the piece of gingham.

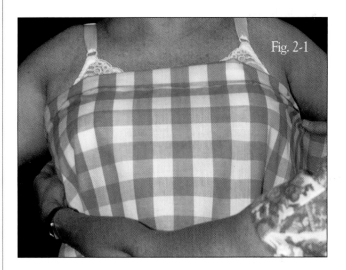

Fig. 2-1

Wrap a single length of gingham around the body from behind the left arm to behind the right arm.

*To mark muslin, first draw a vertical line down the center of the fabric, parallel to the selvage. Then, draw a perpendicular line across the width of the fabric, in the center. Draw horizontal lines across the width of the fabric at 4-inch intervals from this perpendicular line, making sure they are 4 inches apart on either side of the centerline. Continue these lines the length of the fabric.

CUT A NECK OPENING

You need to cut a neck opening in the center of the gingham which should be as close to the subject's actual neck size as is possible, erring on the side of being wider rather than narrower. To determine the proper size, place the weighted rope or necklace on the neck and have the subject situate it comfortably, as a necklace would be worn. Pull the two sides down vertically, so that they are parallel to each other from the neck down, and measure the width between each outside edge of the rope, to the nearest 1/8th inch (Fig. 2-2). This is the neck width. Refer to Fig. 2-3, the Neckline Template, and select the appropriate neckline width that is equal to or greater than the subject's own.* For example, if the subject's neck width was 5-3/8 inches, you'd choose the 5-1/2-inch-wide neckline. Divide this measurement by 2 to get the half (pattern total) neck width, and record this measurement on the Pattern Drafting Personal Measurement Chart under "front neck width."

If your subject's neck width is not listed on the template, draw your own correct neckline using the template as an example of neckline shape.

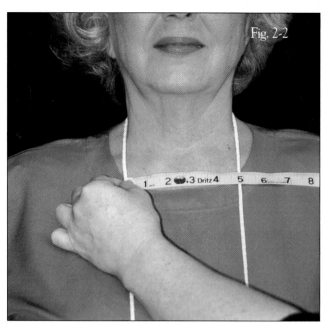

Pull the sides of the weighted rope down vertically and measure between the outside edges. This is the front neck width.

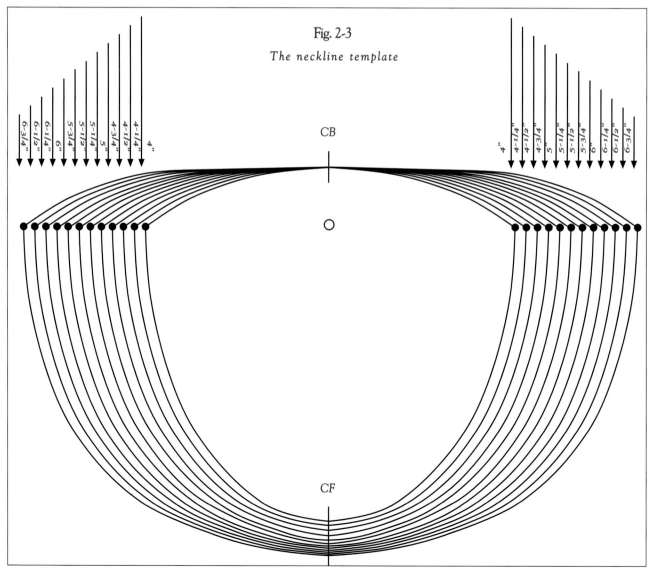

Fig. 2-3

The neckline template

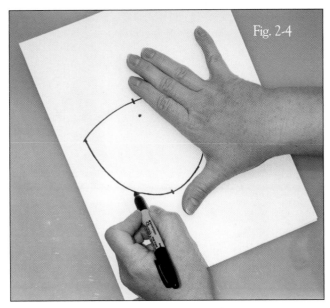

Make a neck template by copying the appropriate neckline onto a piece of tracing paper. Trace the properly sized neckline, the center dot, center front, center back, and neck point markings.

Make a neck template by copying the appropriate neckline, the center dot, CF, center back (CB), and neck point markings onto a piece of tracing paper (Fig. 2-4). Now cut the neckline out, right along the actual line, so you have a roughly oval piece of paper with the division markings on it. Open out the gingham and lay the neck oval over the gingham's center, aligning the center dots and making sure that the neck points are on the same cross grain line. Trace around the template with a marking pen, and mark the CF, CB, and both neck points onto the gingham (Fig. 2-5). Cut out the neck opening exactly on this marked line, and cut a 5 to 7-inch slit straight down center front, so the gingham will fit over the head. Make absolutely sure that the neck size is not too tight. It's okay for it to be too big, because during the course of Bodymapping you will take note of the difference between where the "necklace" sits and where the gingham ends. Save this neckline template; you'll use it in the pattern drafting stage.

TRIM AWAY THE ARMHOLE EXCESS

The last step in preparing the gingham is to trim away some of the fabric in the shoulder/upper arm area. Fold the gingham along the cross grain line that has the neck point markings. Fold it again along the center front. Count over from each neck point about 8 inches (8 squares on 1-inch gingham). From there, draw a rough armhole curve that ends at the edge of the gingham, about 8 inches below the folded cross grain line (Fig. 2-6). Don't bother to use a French curve at this point—it's not necessary because you will eventually trim away much more fabric around the armhole. Trim away the fabric outside of the curve.

DELINEATE THE SUBJECT'S "LANDMARKS"

Tie the bottom of the weighted rope loosely at the ends so it will stay put. Now you need to delineate a few points on the subject's body with the stick-on dots and the narrow tape. To find the neck point, feel for the tendon at the side of the neck

Trace around the neck template with a marking pen onto the gingham

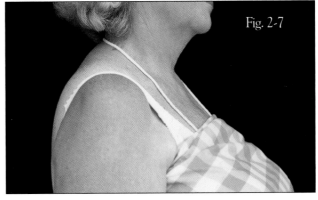

Place a stick-on dot at each neck point.

Draw a rough armhole on the gingham and trim away the excess fabric.

that rises as the head is tilted over to the opposite side; usually this will be directly under or just behind the center of the earlobe (1/2 inch or so). Put a stick-on dot in this position, on each side of the neck (Fig. 2-7). The dots should be right to the outside of the weighted rope, or very slightly under it. Place the end of a piece of tape next to the neck point dot at the neck's base. The other end of the tape goes straight out to the shoulder tip (or bone) (Fig. 2-8). Observing the subject from the side, the tape would, if it continued down the arm, visually bisect the upper arm. Do both sides. It's imperative that the shoulder lines be delineated properly, for their placement in the finished garment is crucial to the balance and comfort of that garment. Feel for the ridge of bone where the arm socket fits into the shoulder bone; this is the natural shoulder point. Now place a stick-on dot where the tape intersects this point on each side.

Next, place a 15 to 20 inch line of tape along each side of the body, vertically down from a few inches below the armpit to the hip level (Fig. 2-9). These markings delineate the side seam placement. Place a stick-on dot at the point where the backbone meets the weighted rope (Fig. 2-10). This delineates the center back neck point. Place a piece of narrow elastic around the waist and have the subject tie it and situate it comfortably, as a waistband would fit. It's not necessary for the elastic to be completely horizontal—it should be worn as a pant or skirt waistband is worn, and this position varies from person to person.

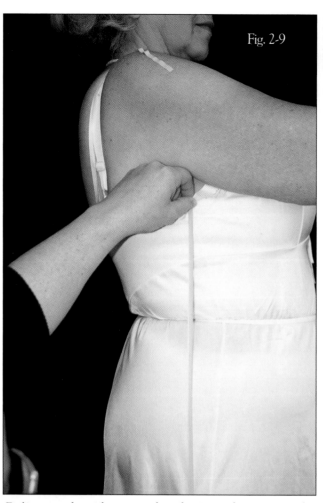

Delineate the side seams by placing a long strip of tape vertically on the side of the body from the underarm to the hip level.

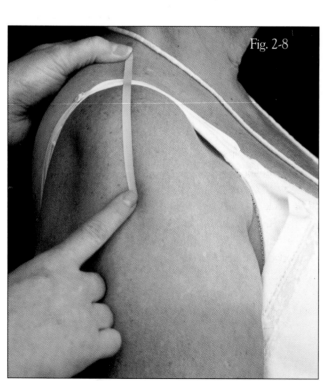

Delineate the shoulder line by extending a piece of tape from the neck point to the middle of the upper arm.

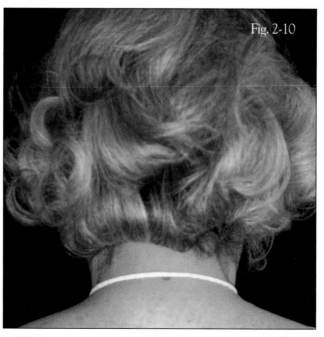

Delineate the CB neck point by placing a stick-on dot at the point where the backbone meets the weighted rope.

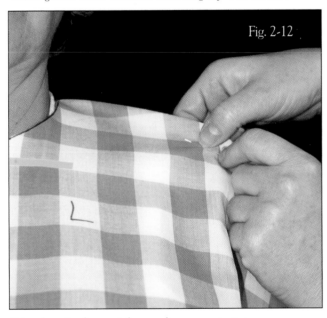

Raise the gingham until it appears completely smooth from the neck to the outside edge with the cross grain lines neither slanting up nor down.

Pin the gingham right at the exact point your fingers are pinching. Pin parallel to the shoulder line.

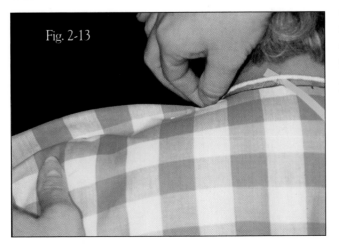

THE BODYMAPPING PROCESS

With the slit in front, place the Bodymap over the subject's head, like a poncho. Situate the back of the neck first, aligning the center back mark on the gingham with the stick-on dot at the subject's center back neck. Tape the gingham in place with a narrow piece of masking tape. It is critical that, throughout the Bodymapping process, the subject is standing relaxed, with legs straight and even and arms resting comfortably.

Situate the front part of the neckline with the slit opening at CF. Tape the gingham shut at the highest comfortable level, making sure that the gingham does not overlap or gap open. Sometimes the highest level is below the top edge of the gingham. That's okay, just tape it securely and let the top gently fold over. Pin the tape to the gingham if necessary.

Check the side of the neckline to make sure that the gingham doesn't show *inside* of the weighted rope, which would indicate a neckline that's too small. If it does, remove the gingham, trace the next larger sized neckline, and re-cut the gingham's neckline. It's okay if the gingham lies outside of the weighted rope, because any difference will be noted and corrected in the pattern drafting stage.

Mark the left and right sides of the Bodymap on both the front and the back.

PIN THE SHOULDER SLOPE DARTS

Standing in front of the subject's left shoulder, insert your right hand into the fold at the top of the gingham. Raise the gingham until it appears completely smooth from the neck to the outside edge, with the cross grain lines slanting neither up nor down (Fig. 2-11).

Pinch the gingham as close to the taped shoulder line on the top of the shoulder as possible, at the approximate position of the shoulder bone. Remove your right hand, grab a pin, and insert it parallel to the plane of the skin at the exact point your fingers are pinching the gingham (Fig. 2-12).

Standing in back of the subject's left shoulder, pinch the excess fabric that lies over the middle of the shoulder and pin it, again parallel to the shoulder (Fig. 2-13). Move your left hand towards the neck and pin the excess fabric just outside of the neck point, approximately 1/2 inch away. Pin away from the neck, from right to left. At this point, you should only be pinching out a scant 1/4 to 1/2 inch. Because the folded edge of the gingham will not allow a shifting of fabric, sometimes the shoulder slope darts tend to slant towards the back of the neck, behind the marked neck point. Don't worry about this.

Back view of the pinned shoulder slope darts.

Standing behind the subject's right shoulder, raise and pin the gingham as you did the left side. Next, pin the excess in the middle of the shoulder. Move around to the front of the subject's right side and pin the gingham near the neck point. You may pin out more or less at this neck point compared to the other side, indicating an asymmetrical shoulder slope, which is extremely common.

Stand back and observe the subject's back from a few feet away. The top portion of the gingham should appear smooth and symmetrical from side to side (Fig. 2-14), with the cross grain lines either parallel to the floor (for a very straight posture) or slanting very gently down from the neck points to the shoulders (for an average posture), and the center back should be perfectly vertical. On both the back and front, make sure there are no diagonal folds in the gingham between the shoulder points and above the mid-armholes. There should be no gaping at either neck point. The pins should be right on top of the taped shoulder line at the shoulder point, but if they're slightly to one side, disregard it, because you'll double-check the shoulder positions at the end of the process.

PIN THE BUST DARTS

Stand slightly to the right front side of the subject, and, with your left hand, raise the side of the gingham at about bust level straight out so that the cross grain line is parallel to the floor. Smooth it around to the side of the body as if wrapping the corner of a box. Pin it temporarily to the undergarment at the side of the body, in line with the taped side seam, about 3 inches below the underarm (Fig. 2-15). Disregard the excess fabric that forms in the armhole area diagonally up from the bust point.

The point (like the corner on a box) where the gingham turns down and to the side is the bust point. Have the subject place a stick-on dot at this position or mark it with a pen (Fig. 2-16). If, in profile, the subject's abdomen protrudes much farther than the bust, it will be impossible to bring the cross grain line to a horizontal level at the side of the body under the arm without pulling the center front off-balance (Fig. 2-17). This is because there is a much larger width and length of fabric needed to encompass the abdomen than to encompass the bust, and this situation presents a unique challenge when trying to fit a garment that is one piece from top to bottom, with no waistline seam. This type of figure must have an additional fitting line in order to accommodate the drastic

Have the subject place a stick-on dot or pen mark on the bust point.

Stand back and observe the shoulder area.

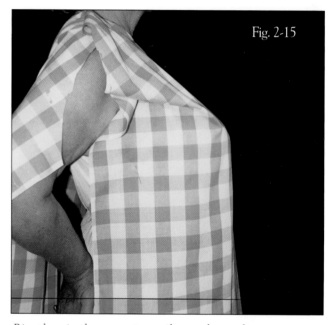

Pin the gingham temporarily to the undergarment at the side of the body, allowing excess fabric to form in the armhole area.

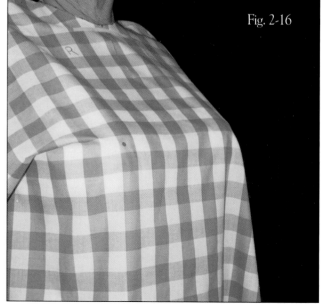

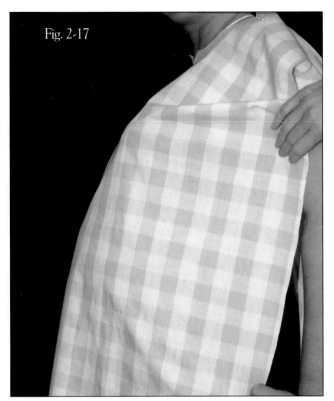

Fig. 2-17

If, in profile, the subject's abdomen protrudes farther than the bust, it will be impossible to bring the cross grain line to a horizontal level at the side of the body under the arm without pulling the CF off balance.

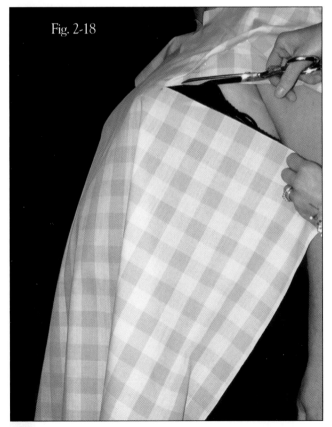

Fig. 2-18

Cut into the gingham horizontally at the approximate cross grain line that crosses the bust point, cutting just to the bust point.

difference from top to bottom. Because we're concentrating on garments without a waistline seam, a vertical style line (or princess line) garment is a requirement for this particular body type in order to maintain perfectly horizontal grain lines at the hem. There is an additional step in the Bodymapping process that this body type requires at this point. If your subject does not have a protruding abdomen, and your cross grain line moved smoothly into the horizontal position at the side underarm, skip the next paragraph and move on.

If your subject does have a protruding abdomen, cut into the gingham horizontally at the exact cross grain line that crosses the bust point, cutting just to the bust point (Fig. 2-18). Now smooth the gingham from the side seam to the bust point so that the cut edges are aligned and the cross grain line is perfectly horizontal. Tape the cut edges together so they're secure. Pin out the extra fabric, usually between 1/2 to 2 inches total, right under the bust point (Fig. 2-19).

Move to the subject's left side, and with your right hand, lift and smooth the gingham to the left underarm area, keeping the cross grain line parallel to the floor. Pin the gingham temporarily as you did the right side and mark the bust point as you did the right side. Staying on the left side, insert your right hand into the fold formed by the excess fabric which has

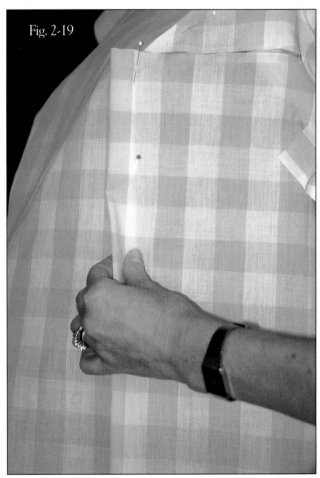

Fig. 2-19

Pin out the extra fabric that forms directly under the bust point.

formed in the left armhole area. With your left hand, pinch the fabric right next to the armhole, in the crease that forms at the junction of the torso and left arm. Remove your right hand, grab a pin, and insert it from right to left exactly at this point, going from the armhole towards the bust point (Fig. 2-20). The pin must be right against the plane of the skin, without causing the fabric to strain. Move down towards the bust about 2 inches and pin out the excess fabric that has formed there as well. The excess fabric will automatically taper to nothing at the bust point so there's no need to pin closer to it. Do the other side, making sure to pin from the outside in so the pin doesn't poke the subject's arm. Stand back and evaluate your grain lines, which should be level (Fig. 2-21). The fabric should lie smoothly over the bust with no diagonal folds, evident strain, or excess width.

On each side, look under the gingham's edge to locate the crease that forms where the arm meets the torso and place a dot or pen mark here (Fig. 2-22). This is the front draping point, the location where the front of the body becomes the side of the body. If the subject seems to have more than one crease, place your dot at the point where the creases converge and start to go under the arm. Trace the outline of the armhole for 1-1/2 to 2 inches below this point. Clip into the marked armholes once or twice so the fabric will lay smoothly (Fig. 2-23).

Have the subject place a fingertip at the base of the bust, where it meets the ribcage. Mark this point with a horizontal line. This will be use to determine the bust radius (Fig. 2-24).

PIN THE UPPER BACK DARTS

The point where the gingham turns down and to the side

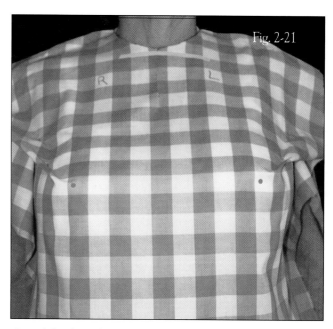

Stand back and evaluate your grain lines from a distance, which should be level.

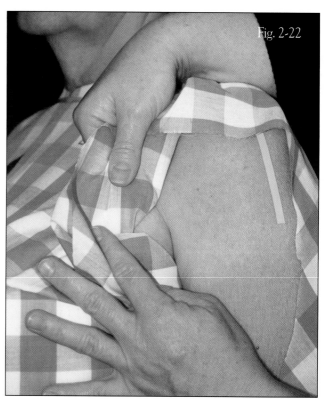

Peek under the gingham's edge to locate the crease that forms where the arm meets the torso.

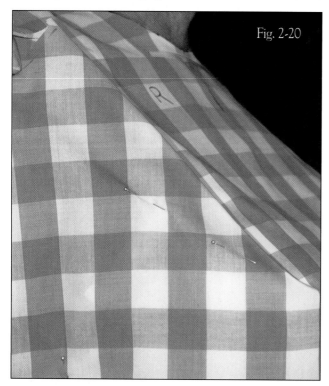

Close-up of a properly pinned bust dart

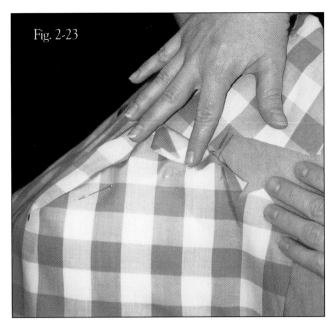

Trace the outline of the armholes for 1-1/2 to 2 inches below the front draping point and clip into the marked armholes once or twice so the fabric will lie smoothly.

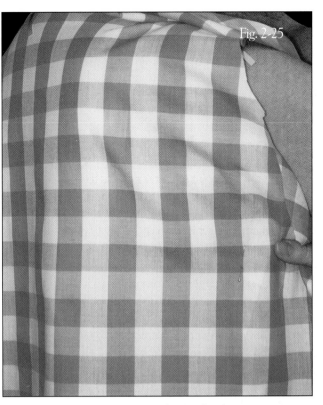

Pin the gingham temporarily to the front section, a few inches below the underarm.

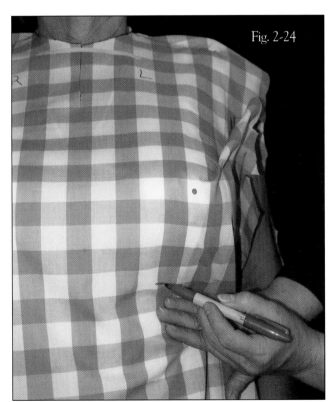

With a horizontal line, mark the point where the base of the bust*meets the ribcage. The is the bust radius, which will be used in pattern drafting.

If, in profile, the subject's buttocks protrude past the upper back, it may be impossible to bring the cross grain line to a horizontal level at the side of the body under the arm without pulling the CB off balance.

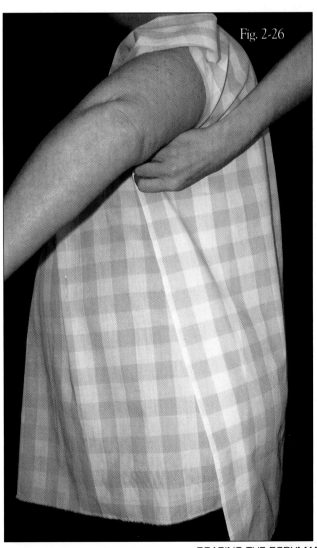

is the apex of the upper back curve. Mark this point with a pen mark at each side of the back. Stand slightly to the right back side of the subject, and, with your right hand, raise the gingham out to the side so that the cross grain line at the approximate underarm level is parallel to the floor (Fig. 2-25). Smooth it around to the side of the body as you did the front and pin it temporarily to the front section, below the underarm, keeping the cross grain line parallel to the floor. If, in profile, the subject's buttocks protrude an inordinate amount past the upper back, it may be impossible for the cross grain line to a horizontal level at the side of the body under the arm without pulling the center back off balance (Fig. 2-26).

This is because there is a much larger width and length of fabric needed to encompass the buttocks than the upper back, and this situation presents a unique problem when trying to fit a garment that is one piece from top to bottom, with no waistline seam. As in the case of a protruding abdomen previously mentioned, this type of figure must have an additional fitting line in order to accommodate the drastic difference from top to bottom. Follow the procedure for the protruding abdomen, cutting the fabric just below the level of and just to the upper back curve (Fig. 2-27). Pin out the extra fabric that has formed right under the edge of the cut fabric.

Make sure that you haven't pulled the center back off-grain; it should still hang vertically. Do the other side and double-check that both the lengthwise and crosswise grain lines are in their proper positions.

Next, standing behind the subject's right shoulder, feel, with your finger, the crease that forms where the arm meets the torso. With both hands, pinch out whatever excess fabric forms at this crease.

Holding the pinched fabric with your left thumb and forefinger, remove your right hand, grab a pin, and pin the excess fabric (usually about 3/4 to 1 inch total) out exactly at the pinched position (Fig. 2-28). Pin from right to left. The dart will taper to zero at the apex of the upper back curve, which could be close to the backbone, in the case of a dowager's hump (Fig. 2-29). This point will be referred to as "shoulder blade point," but may not be on the actual shoulder blade tip. Pin the dart at least once more along its length, to the point where it tapers to nothing. A very straight back may have only a scant 3/8 to 1/2 inch pinned out at the armhole,

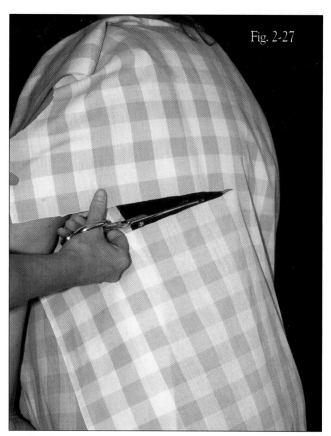

Fig. 2-27

Cut the fabric below the level of the underarm horizontally to a point that's directly below the fullest part of the upper back.

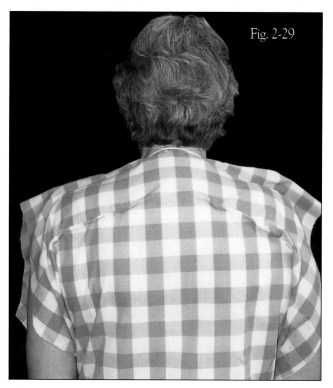

Fig. 2-29

A dart that tapers to zero close to the backbone indicates a dowager's hump.

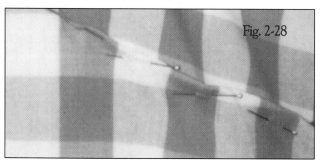

Fig. 2-28

Pinch out the excess fabric that forms in the area where the arm meets the torso and pin it until it tapers to zero.

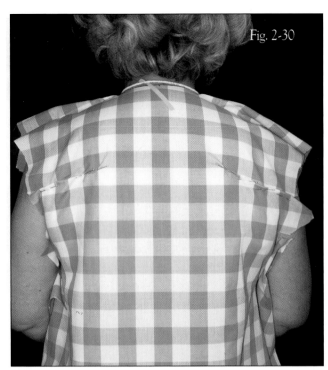

Fig. 2-30

Stand back and evaluate your grain lines. The fabric should lie smoothly over the upper back with no diagonal folds or evident strain.

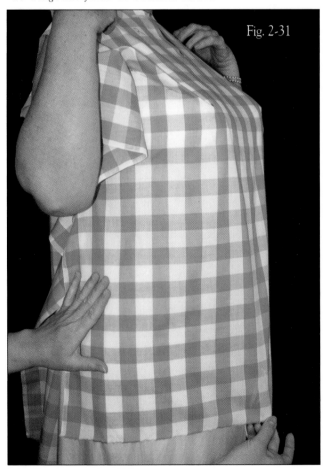

Fig. 2-31

Facing the right front of the subject, hold the center front of the gingham at the very bottom of the cloth and keep it in its vertical position as you pick up the side edge of the gingham with your left hand at about hip level.

whereas a dowager humped back may have as much as 1-1/2 inches or more.

Do the other side, making sure to pin from the outside in so the pin doesn't poke the subject's arm. Stand back and evaluate your grain lines. The fabric should lie smoothly over the upper back with no diagonal folds, evident strain, or excess width (Fig. 2-30).

The gingham's center back should hang vertically, and the cross grain line should be horizontal below the newly pinned upper back darts. Locate and mark the draping points and armholes as you did on the front.

PIN THE SIDE SEAMS

You're going to start at the bottom of the cloth for this step, so sit down or have the subject step up to a level where your eye is even with the subject's hip. Facing the right front of the subject, hold the center front of the gingham at the very bottom of the cloth and keep it in its vertical position as you pick up the side edge of the gingham with your left hand, at about hip level (Fig. 2-31).

Smooth the gingham to the side until its cross grain line is horizontal, and temporarily pin it to the subject's undergarment (Fig. 2-32).

It's important to note that there may appear to be, on some subjects, excess fabric from below the bust points all the way to the hem line, even if you're sure the cross grain line at both sides is exactly horizontal. This extra fabric is there for a very good reason—the top of the subject is considerably larger

Fig. 2-32

Smooth the gingham to the side and pin it temporarily to the subject's undergarment.

than the bottom of the subject—in the front, at least. When you reach the last step (pinning the waist darts) you'll continue pinning fabric all the way down from the bust to the hem line, rather than fading to zero at the fullest part of the tummy or hip. More about this when we reach the waist dart section.

Do the other side of the front, making sure that the center front of the gingham is still hanging vertically.

Now, turn the subject around so that you're facing the right back of the body. Hold the center back of the gingham at the bottom of the cloth with your left hand, and pick up the edge of the gingham with your right hand at approximately the level of the full hip. Hold it out so its cross grain line is horizontal and wrap it around to the side. Pin it temporarily to the front section (Fig. 2-33).

Move to the left back side of the subject and repeat the process, this time holding the center back of the gingham with your right hand and lifting and smoothing the left side of the gingham with your left hand. Step back and evaluate your grain lines from the back, front, and from each side, making sure the center front and center back are vertical and the cross grain lines are horizontal at the hip level.

Where the two edges are pinned together, the back's squares may or may not line up with the front's squares, but the left and right side should be symmetrical. For instance, if the left front meets the hem line of the left back 2-1/2 squares above the front hem line, then the right front should meet the hem line of the right back 2-1/2 squares above the front hem line. Double-check this now and adjust if needed. Pin the two edges together securely, aligning the pins with the imaginary extension of the taped side seam. Pin from top to bottom.

Stand to the right side of the subject and pin the side seams together, about every 3 or 4 inches, all the way up the side. Stop about 3 inches below the underarm.

Do the left side of the subject as well. You may have to fine-tune this step by alternating from side to side so that you make sure the center front and center back are not being pulled out of their proper positions. Make sure that the two sides are joining with the same square-relationship all the way up, as they did at the bottom. For example, if the bottom of the blue square on the front meets the middle of a white square on the back, maintain this relationship all the way up, keeping the lengthwise grain line vertical and therefore the crosswise grain line horizontal (Fig. 2-34). An easy way to check this is by opening the pinned seam as if it were a pressed open seam worn inside out.

Clip into the fabric in the armhole area a few more times if needed, so that the fabric lies smoothly, and trim away the excess. Pin the side seam higher, stopping about 2 inches below the underarm level.

Now that you're sure you have enough gingham to go around the largest circumference of the body, trim away the excess fabric on the outside of each pinned side seam. Leave about an inch extra (1-inch seam allowance) on the outside

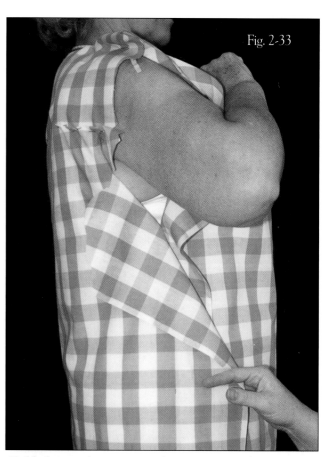

Hold the gingham out so the cross grain line is horizontal at the hip level and pin it temporarily to the front section.

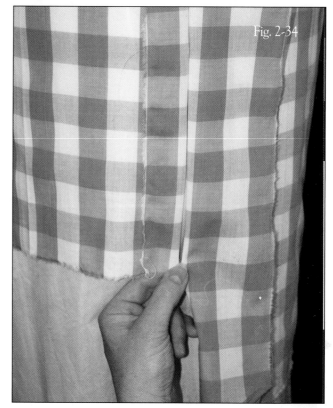

Double-check that the left and right side seams are joined with the same square relationship by opening the pinned seam as if it were a pressed open seam worn inside out.

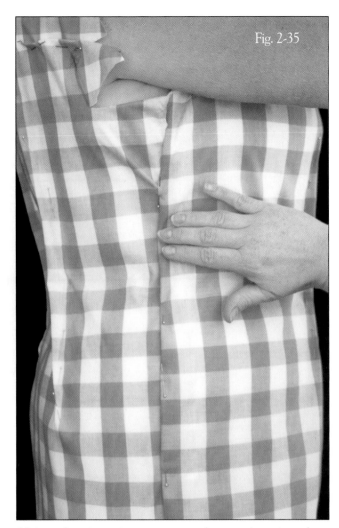

Fig. 2-35

If it makes it easier to ensure that you've pinned the side seam correctly, re-pin the side seams with the raw edge folded under.

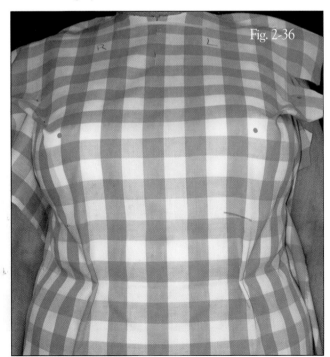

Fig. 2-36

Pinch out any excess fabric that may exist below the bust points at the level of the waist elastic.

of the pinned seam line on both the front and back. Where applicable, trim off the excess fabric from the hem line on whichever side is longer (usually the back), making sure the side seams meet exactly at the hem. If you'd like to neaten up your side seams and confirm that the Bodymap is joined correctly at the sides, you can re-pin the side seams with the raw edges under. To do this, starting at the bottom, pin on the right side, release it, fold under the back seam allowance, and re-pin it to the front in the exact same position (Fig. 2-35). Do this all the way up and on both sides.

Step back and evaluate your grain lines. Measure from each side seam hem line to the floor with a yardstick (not a tape measure). They should measure the same. If they don't, either the gingham is off-grain or you have a problem with your grain controlling darts—most likely either the shoulder slope dart or the bust dart, or a combination of the two. Whatever the case, make the hem line level by deepening (adding more take-up to) the darts on the lower side, even though the cross grain lines in the dart area may then appear slightly diagonal. These imbalances will be resolved during the drafting of the base pattern.

PIN OUT THE WAIST DARTS

Stand directly in front of the subject and, with both hands, pinch out any excess fabric that may exist below the bust points at the level of the waist elastic, trying to pinch a similar amount on either side.

Make sure this step doesn't cause any diagonal pulls to

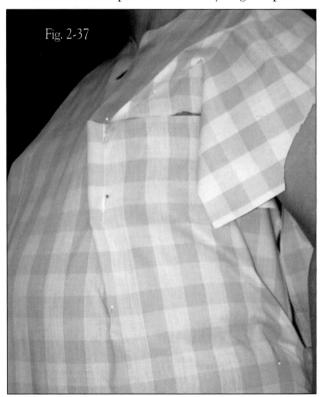

Fig. 2-37

If you performed the protruding abdomen steps, the waist dart will taper to whatever amount you have pinned out just below the bust point, so pin it smoothly from waist to bust.

form. If it does, you've pinched out too much fabric at the waist and will need to release a bit. Release the right side temporarily, grab a pin, and pin the left waist dart right on top of the waist elastic, with the pin going in from top to bottom. Now pin the right side in the same manner (Fig. 2-36). Pin the waist darts again once or twice at midriff level, just below the base of the bust. If you performed the protruding abdomen steps above, the (usually very small) waist dart will taper to whatever amount you have pinned out just below the bust point, so pin it smoothly from waist to bust (Fig. 2-37).

Now pin below the waist by pinching out any excess fabric that occurs below the waist dart. It may taper to zero within 2 or 3 inches, or within 8 or 9 inches, or you may pinch out fabric all the way down to the hem line without it ever tapering to zero. Just make sure you're pinching out enough fabric to make the gingham rest smoothly on the body, grain lines correct, with enough room to go around but with no strains or diagonal pulls. Repeat the process in the back below the shoulder blades.

Double-check that the waist elastic is still in a comfortable waistband position, and with a marker, trace over the waistline by feeling the position of the elastic tied around the subject's waist. Make sure to trace the waistline exactly to the side seams so you'll have match-points to use as guidelines for pattern drafting (Fig. 2-38).

DETERMINE THE APPROPRIATE SIZE AND POSITION OF CERTAIN ASPECTS OF THE NECK, SHOULDER, AND ARM

Before starting, double-check the position of the outside

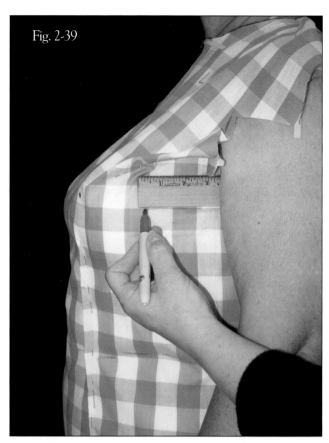

Delineate the underarm level by marking the position of the bottom of the straight edge onto both the front and back of the Bodymap.

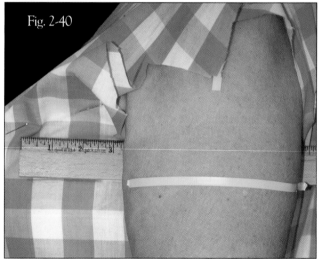

Place a piece of narrow tape at this same level on one arm. This is the bicep line.

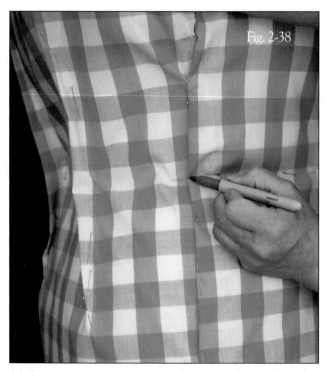

Make sure to trace the waistline exactly to the side seam so you'll have match points to use as guidelines for pattern drafting.

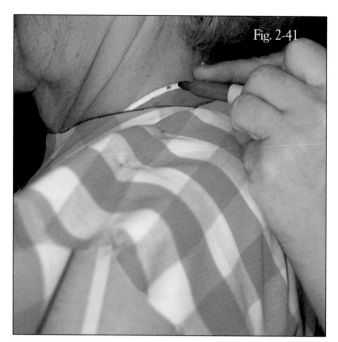

Make a mark on the weighted rope where it crosses the neck point stick-on dots at both sides of the subject's neck.

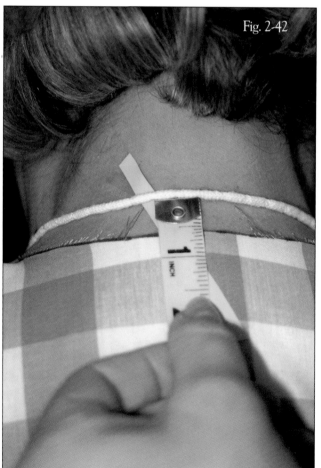

Measure the distance between the gingham's neckline and the weighted rope at the back of the neck.

shoulder pins; they should lie right on top of the marked shoulder bone. If they don't, release and re-pin the shoulder slope darts, allowing the fold of the fabric to taper towards the back of the neck if that's where it wants to. The fabric will naturally want to slide towards the back at this stage. Don't worry if the neck point of the gingham doesn't align with the subject's actual neck point; it's the shoulder point you need to adjust now.

Have the subject position a straight-edge under the arm, parallel to the floor. It should be flush against the underarm without causing any discomfort. Mark the position of the *bottom* of the straight edge onto both the front and the back Bodymap (Fig. 2-39). The mark should extend horizontally for an inch or so, to differentiate it from other markings on the Bodymap. Do both sides of the body. This is the underarm level. Place a piece of narrow tape at this same level on one arm. This is the bicep line (Fig. 2-40).

Make a mark on the weighted rope where it crosses the neck point stick-on dots at both sides of the subject's neck (Fig. 2-41). (If you are using a necklace, mark it with tape or stick on dots at the neck point location.)

Triple-check the position of the shoulder pins and make note of the distance, if any, between the gingham's neckline and the weighted rope (Fig. 2-42). Measure this distance at the back and both sides of the neck and write the amount on the Bodymap.

Mark the position of the front neck by feeling for the base of the tendon as the neck stretches up (Fig. 2-43). This may be above, at, or below the edge of the gingham at center front.

For the next step, determining the garment shoulder seam length, you'll need the shoulder pad. With your left hand, hold a straight-edge so that it lies flush against the middle part

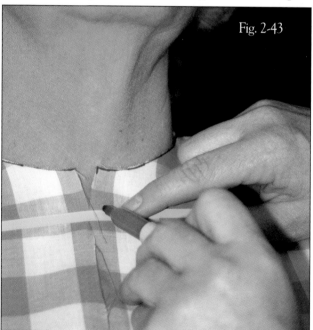

Mark the level of the front neck by feeling the base of the tendon felt as the neck stretches up.

of the subject's upper arm. It should not touch the lower part of the upper arm, near the elbow, nor should it touch the uppermost part of the arm, near the shoulder bone. It should extend up slightly past the shoulder. With your right hand, place the shoulder pad on the shoulder and slide it out so that it touches the straight edge (Fig. 2-44).

Have the subject hold the shoulder pad in this exact position. Remove the straight-edge and, holding the end of a measuring tape at the marked neck point, drape it over the tip of the shoulder pad and let it fall past the taped bicep line. Measure the distances: "A" from the neck point to the tip of the shoulder pad and "B" from the tip of the shoulder pad to the taped bicep line (Fig. 2-45). Do all of the following arm measurements on both sides of the body, choosing the largest measurement if there is a difference.

Remove the weighted rope from the subject and measure the distance between the marked neck points. Write this amount on the Bodymap, labeling it "back neck length." Subtract 1/2 inch from "A" and write this amount on the Bodymap, labeling it "garment shoulder seam length." Then add 1 inch to "B" and write this amount on the Bodymap, labeling it "cap height" (for the set-in sleeve that you'll be drafting).* Record these two measurements in pencil in the Personal Measurement Chart (See the next page).

Next, measure around the arm at the bicep level. Mark this amount on the Bodymap, labeling it "bicep circumference."

Then you'll need to delineate the wrist line. Do this by placing a piece of narrow tape around the subject's wrist, as if it were a tight fitting bracelet.

Measure the front of the arm from the marked bicep line to the wrist line and mark it on the Bodymap, labeling it "front arm length."

Then measure the back of the arm from the bicep to the wrist line, going right over the back of the elbow, making note also of the distance from the bicep line to the bone of the elbow. Mark these amounts on the Bodymap, labeling the first "back arm length" and the second "elbow depth."

Take one final look at the Bodymap from all sides, and if you're satisfied that your grain lines are correct, mark the placement of all the pins clearly with a marking pen. Make sure you mark the positions of the pin centers on both pieces of fabric that are pinned together, with marks that are at least 1/4 inch long running parallel to the pins. By marking all of the pins before removing the Bodymap you'll guard against losing any pin positions should a pin happen to fall out.

Take the Bodymap off the subject and measure the distances from the neck points to the natural shoulder points. Record the larger measurement on the Bodymap as the natural shoulder seam length. Remove the elastic and the stick-on dots from the body.

Transfer all of these measurements from the Bodymap to the Pattern Drafting Personal Measurement Chart.

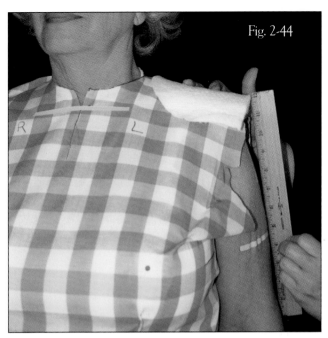

Fig. 2-44

Slide the shoulder pad out so it touches the straight edge.

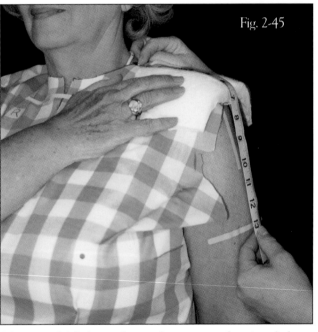

Fig. 2-45

Measure "A" from the neck point to the tip of the shoulder pad and "B" from the tip of the shoulder pad to the taped bicep line.

*If the subject used a thicker shoulder pad than the 1/2 inch specified, add the difference to the cap height determined here.

PATTERN DRAFTING PERSONAL MEASUREMENT CHART

MISCELLANEOUS DRAFTING Measurements:	AMOUNT
A. Front neck width	
B. Back neck length	
C. Bust radius	
D. Bust dart angle	
E. Upper back dart angle	
SLEEVE DRAFTING Measurements:	
F. Cap height	
G. Garment shoulder seam length	
H. Natural shoulder seam length	
I. Bicep circumference	
J. Front arm length	
K. Back arm length	
L. Elbow depth (from bicep line)	
M. Front armhole length	
N. Back armhole length	

CHAPTER 3
MAKING A BASE PATTERN

Quite often, the Bodymap appears to have completely different markings from side to side, for instance, different levels for bust points, a slanted waist dart on one side, uneven shoulder slope darts, etc. These imbalances are often a product of the forgiving nature of the Bodymapping process, rather than evidence of actual differences in shaping requirements from one side to another, but you'll need to determine at some point if body asymmetry does exist. It's quite easy, even on a symmetrical body, for some of the gingham to be molded inadvertently into the shoulder slope dart when it really belongs in the bust dart, for example, and the dart take-up can vary from side to side as well, because you're just "eyeballing," not measuring, when draping the Bodymap. So you must begin the pattern drafting process by measuring, evaluating, and sometimes redistributing the angles of the six grain controlling darts (the bust, shoulder slope, and upper back darts on both the right and left sides). After determining the appropriate dart angle size, you'll trace over all of your pin markings and draft a symmetrical whole pattern for the front and the back. During the drafting process, you'll alternate from pencil (temporary markings) to marking pen (permanent markings).

DRAFTING TERMINOLOGY

You'll need to familiarize yourself with the following drafting terms:

<u>Square a line</u>: Draw a line perpendicular (at 90° or right angles) to another line or point (**Fig. 3-1**). Do this by aligning the right angle's horizontal side along the original line and its vertical side at the point you're squaring from. Trace along the right angle to form the squared line.

<u>Draw a parallel line</u>: Measure out the same distance from both ends of the original line and place a dot at both points. Connect the dots with a straight line (**Fig. 3-2**). The two lines are parallel, or an equal distance apart at every point.

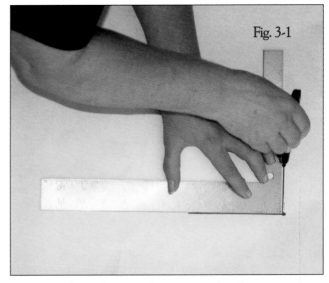

Square a line. Draw a line perpendicular to another line.

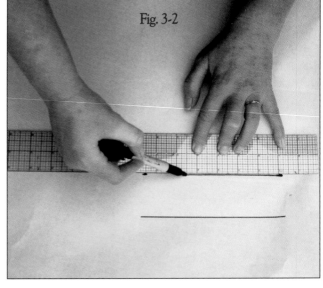

To draw a parallel line, measure out the specific distance from both ends of the original line, dot both points, and connect them with a straight line.

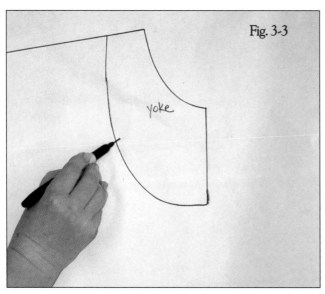

Fig. 3-3

When drafting patterns, cross mark a style line before separating the pattern pieces, so that when you cut them apart each pattern piece will have a match point for sewing.

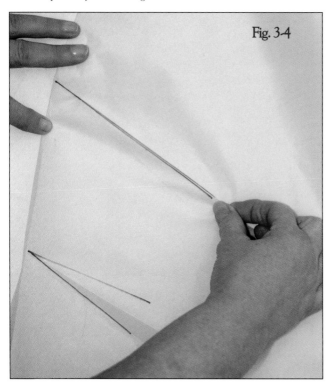

Fig. 3-4

To fold out a dart, crease the fold in the pattern that intersects the dart tip and fold the section of the pattern not containing the dart under. Crease the inside or lower dart leg and bring it to meet the other dart leg. The pattern should lie perfectly flat.

<u>Cross mark</u>: A short (1/4-inch long) line used to indicate the match point of two seam lines. Cross marks are placed at various locations on patterns to ensure the pattern pieces are sewn together as intended (Fig. 3-3). Some commercial pattern companies use triangular notches instead of straight lines. To transfer the triangular notch mark(s) on the cutting line of a commercial pattern to the seam line, bisect the triangle and extend this line to the seam line. To avoid confusion, use a single cross mark on front pattern pieces and double cross marks on back pieces. Never cross mark right in the center of a seam line.

<u>Fold out a dart</u>: Crease the inside (vertical darts) or lower (horizontal darts) dart leg and bring it to meet the other dart leg, closing the dart (Fig. 3-4). To properly fold out a dart, crease a fold in the pattern that intersects the dart tip, and fold under the section of the pattern not containing the dart. Close the dart, just to the dart tip. The dart underlay folds either down or towards the garment center, unless otherwise instructed. The pattern should lie perfectly flat.

<u>True</u>: Make sure that parts of the pattern which are to be sewn together are the correct length and shape and make sure any darts, tucks, or pleats have the appropriately shaped underlay at the seam line. Fold out any darts as noted above and cut the pattern paper along the seam line. When the dart is unfolded, the dart underlay will be shaped properly. Align each pattern piece with its neighboring pattern piece as it will be sewn. Curved pattern sections should be "walked" together inch by inch to ensure proper alignment, and the shorter seam line lengthened so it fits the longer one, assuming they are supposed to be the same length. Use a French curve and a straight edge where needed to draw smooth lines where the pattern pieces join. Truing is done to avoid seams that join at awkward angles and seams that are different lengths when they're supposed to be the same. When truing two diagonal seam lines which move away from a vertical line from top to bottom, the seam line will be slightly shortened; when the seam lines move towards the vertical line, the seam lines will be lengthened. In pattern drafting, all seam lines need to be trued before the draft is complete. Because many French and armhole curves are slightly different in their curves, truing the

armhole can be a bit confusing, so I have included a guideline for the properly shaped armhole which you can refer to when completing your pattern on the following pages (See Fig. 3-5). The base pattern armhole is drawn by connecting three points on both the front and back armhole: the shoulder point, the underarm point, and the armhole diagonal, which is a line that is 45° from the underarm level line. The front diagonal length is usually between 3/4 inch and 1-1/8 inches, and the back is usually slightly longer, between 1 inch and 1-1/2 inches. The armhole may touch or go outside of the draping points, but should not go inside of them, and the front armhole may dip slightly below the underarm level line.

<u>Blend:</u> Blending is another aspect of truing and is the process of redrawing a seam line that has been interrupted. To blend, find the midpoint of the interruption and blend the seam line through this point, or if it's a curve that has been made angled, smooth it out with a French curve (Fig. 3-6).

<u>Balance:</u> Average the distance between two straight or curved lines, so that the lines' relativity to the grain or centerline is the same (Fig. 3-7). Balancing is used, for example, to true the side seam curves of the front and back Bodymap pattern.

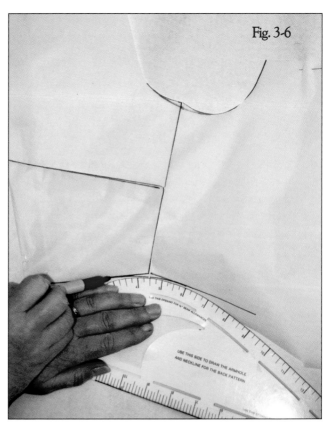

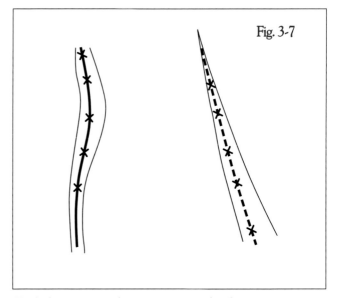

To true a pattern, fold out any darts and align all seam lines together which are to be sewn to each other. Make them the same length by using a straight edge or French curve to join them with smooth lines.

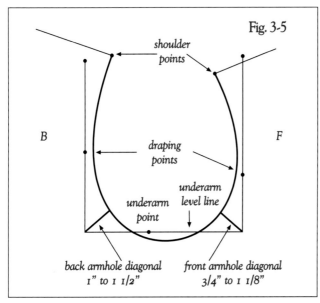

Fig. 3-5

shoulder points

B

F

draping points

underarm level line

underarm point

back armhole diagonal
1" to 1 1/2"

front armhole diagonal
3/4" to 1 1/8"

To blend seam lines, find three points—a starting point, an ending point, and a midpoint, which lies midway between the broken lines—and join these points smoothly with either a French curve or a straight edge.

Fig. 3-7

To balance seam lines, average the distance between them.

Front:

1. Mark CF onto tracing paper and secure it to Bodymap front.
2. Label left and right sides.
3. Mark correct position of CB neck point.
4. Draw the neck point level line (B) at 3/4 inch from CB neck point.
5. Refer to "front neck width" on chart and mark each neck point position on Line B.
6. Draw in temporary shoulder slope darts, bust darts, and upper back darts.
7. Mark each dart at 3 inches from its endpoint and measure and record dart angles.
8. Draw in waist darts.
9. Trace over all markings and remove Bodymap from table.
10. Evaluate and decide on dart angles.
11. Fold paper along CF and secure to table.
12. Measure and record bust radius.
13. Square a line to CF at highest levels of: neck, draping point, bust point, underarm level, waistline/CF junction, waist dart endpoint, and hem line.
14. Average BP position and draw waist dart centerline from here to hem.
15. Average waist dart take-up and draw in correct positions.
16. Average side seams.
17. Average draping points.
18. Draw in the corrected bust darts.
19. Measure and record the completed bust dart angle.
20. Trace over highest front shoulder line and draw in correct shoulder slope dart angle, ending the lines at natural shoulder seam length from personal measurement chart.
21. Fold out bust dart and draw in corrected front armhole, placing an X inside a circle at underarm point.
22. Mark, measure, and record front armhole width.
23. Draw in neckline using neck template.
24. Transfer markings to other side of pattern if desired.

Back:

25. Separate the front and back of the pattern along Line B and set front part aside.
26. Tape paper with Line B onto back of Bodymap, with CB neck point in correct position.
27. Mark CB onto tracing paper and secure it to Bodymap back.
28. Label left and right sides.
29. Trace over back shoulder seam lines, Line B, and back neckline.
30. Measure length of back neckline and change if necessary.
31. Trace over all markings.
32. Remove Bodymap and fold paper along CB marking.
33. Square a line to CB at highest levels of: shoulder blade point, draping point, waistline/CB junction, waist dart endpoint, and hem line. Pencil in back underarm level.
34. Average shoulder blade position and draw in waist dart centerline from here to hem line.
35. Average draping points, side seams, and lower waist darts.
36. Mark underarm point as on front.
37. Draw in temporary armhole.
38. Cut paper at hem line.
39. Draw in the corrected upper back darts.
40. Measure and record the completed upper back dart angle.
41. Mark, measure, and record back armhole width.
42. Draw in corrected back armhole.
43. Transfer markings to other side of pattern, if desired.

Completion:

44. Check whole pattern's length balance and shoulder slope dart angle.
45. Check and adjust armhole widths as needed.
46. Measure and adjust the front and back armholes, if needed.
47. Draw in averaged side seam lines.
48. True underarm curve and cross mark the side waist points.
49. Extend shoulder line to garment length and add shoulder pad allowance.
50. True armholes and neckline and record any change in shoulder seam lengths in Pattern Drafting Personal Measurement Chart.
51. Transfer bust and upper back darts to their proper positions.
52. Correct pattern for protruding abdomen or buttocks, if necessary.
53. Draft sleeve pattern.

DETERMINE THE DART ANGLES

Tear off a piece of tracing paper a few inches larger than the front of the Bodymap, at least 48 inches long, crease it vertically in the center, and draw a line right on the crease. Label this line CF. Remove the tracing paper and lay out the Bodymap front, keeping the back attached to the front but folded up on the table. If you performed either the protruding abdomen or protruding buttocks adjustment, tape the slit portion of the Bodymap together as it was originally, so it lays flat. Secure the Bodymap to the table with tape and then lay the tracing paper over the Bodymap, aligning the CF marking with the center front of the Bodymap and making sure that the tracing paper and the center front line covers the Bodymap from the upper back dart markings to the front hem. Secure the tracing paper to the table with tape, making sure that it's not able to shift, and transfer the "left" and "right" markings onto the tracing paper (Fig. 3-8).

You may notice at this step that your gingham is off-grain after all, evidenced by cross grain lines that are not quite perpendicular to the center front line (Fig. 3-9). If so, any asymmetry determination becomes suspect and should be disregarded, with a check for asymmetry done at the fitting of the first garment made from these pattern drafts.

You may notice that your gingham is off-grain, which makes asymmetry determinations suspect.

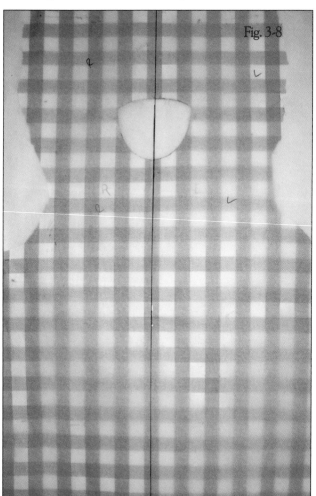

Lay the tracing paper over the Bodymap front with centerlines aligned. Secure the tracing paper to the Bodymap and mark the left and right sides.

Make the correct CB neck position onto the tracing paper. In this example, the corrected neck point was plus 5/8 inch, so the CB neck point was placed 5/8 inch closer to the neck center than the gingham's edge

First, as a reference point, mark the approximate neck center with a pencil by placing a dot in the middle of the oval opening in the gingham. Determine the correct position of the center back neck and place a dot at this level on the extended center front line. For example, if the gingham is

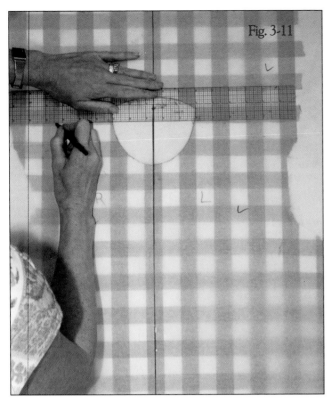

Fig. 3-11

Draw line "B," the neck point level line, perpendicular to the CF line and 3/4 inch closer to the neck center dot than the CB neck point.

Fig. 3-12

Mark the neck points on Line B on both sides of the centerline. Here, the neck width is 5 inches, so the draft total is 2-1/2 inches.

marked "plus 5/8 inch" at the location of the center back neck, mark the tracing paper 5/8 inch closer to the neck center and label it "CB neck point" (Fig. 3-10). If there is not a correction, simply mark the CB neck point at the gingham's edge onto the tracing paper.

From the CB neck point, move towards the neck center 3/4 inch and square a line from the CF line at this level, extending out a few inches past the gingham's neck edge on both sides (Fig. 3-11). Label this line B. Line B indicates the level, almost always, of the neck points as related to the center back neck. Any difference, usually not more than 1/4 inch, can be corrected easily at the fitting of the first garment.

Refer to the Pattern Drafting Personal Measurement Chart, front neck width. On Line B, move out this amount from the CF line on each side and place a dot at each point (Fig. 3-12). These dots indicate the side neck points, referred to from now on as "neck points."

Now, using a pencil, draw in some temporary shoulder seam lines by connecting each corrected neck point to its corresponding shoulder pin markings (the outer most ones) on both front and back. Draw straight lines, disregarding any pin markings at mid-shoulder that may lie outside of the resulting angles. Mark the shoulder seam endpoints (Fig. 3-13) by referring to the Pattern Drafting Personal Measurement Chart, natural shoulder seam length.

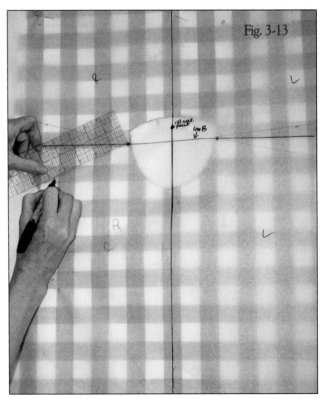

Fig. 3-13

Mark the shoulder seam endpoints by referring to the Personal Measurement Chart. Here, the shoulder seam length is 4-3/4 inches, so the endpoints are marked 4-3/4 inches from each neck point

Now, draw in some temporary bust dart and upper back dart angles as well, also in pencil, by connecting the marked bust and shoulder blade points to the pin markings at each armhole (Fig. 3-14).

Measure each of the six angles, starting with the shoulder slope. To do this, set your compass at 3 inches and place the point of it on one of the corrected neck points. Make an arc which touches both the front and back temporary shoulder seam lines at exactly 3 inches from the neck point (Fig. 3-15). With a measuring tape, measure the distance between the front and back shoulder seam lines at the points of the arc's intersection (Fig. 3-16). Write the measurement down inside the dart angle. Do the same for the remaining five darts and record the amounts for both the right and left sides in the dart angle comparison chart.

DART ANGLE COMPARISON CHART

Right bust	Left bust
Right shoulder slope	Left shoulder slope
Right upper back	Left upper back
Total:	

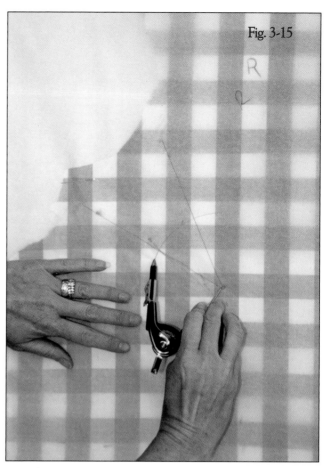

Fig. 3-15

Set the compass at 3 inches, place its point on the pivot point (either the neck point, the bust point (shown here), or the shoulder blade point), and draw an arc which connects the two dart legs.

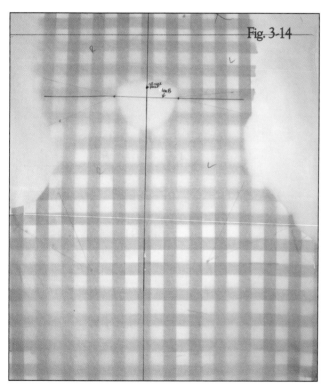

Fig. 3-14

Draw in temporary bust and upper back darts by connecting the bust and shoulder blade points to the pin markings at the corresponding armhole.

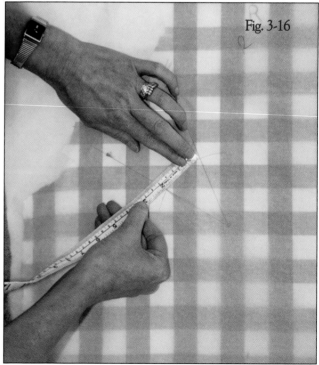

Fig. 3-16

Measure the straight distance between the arc/dart leg intersections.

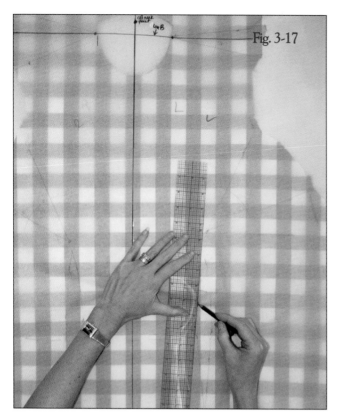

Fig. 3-17

Draw in the bottom half of the waist darts in pencil by connecting the waist level (widest) markings with the lowermost (narrowest) markings.

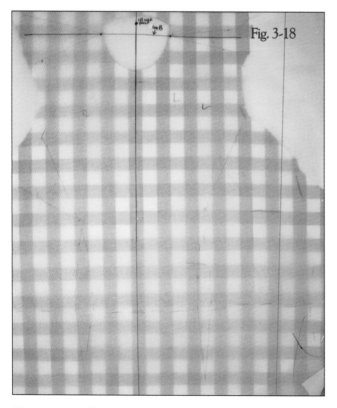

Trace over all pin markings on the front of the Bodymap.

Although they're sometimes equal, it's not uncommon to have a variance between the right and left darts at this stage, which could indicate either an asymmetry of the body or simply different amounts of fabric shifted into certain darts on either side. There is, after all, a fair amount of play allowed in the distribution of these darts.

After you've recorded the amounts on the measurement chart, draw the waist darts in pencil by connecting the waist level (widest) markings with the uppermost and lowermost (narrowest) markings, this time connecting any and all markings, no matter how cock-eyed the darts may appear (Fig. 3-17). (If your subject required that you continued pinning out fabric all the way to the hem line, connect the waist level markings to the point where the marks reach their narrowest and then continue at roughly the same distance apart to the hem line. Connect the hem line markings with straight lines into the waist dart.) If you performed the protruding abdomen adjustment during the draping stage, make sure to trace over the dart markings just below the bust.

Now, with a pencil, trace over all markings on the front of the Bodymap, including the pin markings and those for the front neck level, bust points, waistline, underarm levels, armholes, bust radius, draping points, and hem line (Fig. 3-18).

ANALYZE THE GRAIN-CONTROLLING DART ANGLES

Compare the right side of the body to the left by adding the dart angles together, per side. For example:

Right bust	2-1/4"	Left bust	2"
Right shoulder slope	2-3/4"	Left shoulder slope	3"
Right upper back	1"	Left upper back	3/4"
	6"		5-3/4"

If you discovered that your gingham was off-grain, or if the total difference between the right and left sides is 1/4 inch or less, which probably indicates that one side was just pinned closer to the body than the other, disregard the *larger* angles and circle the smaller ones to use as your corrected dart angles. Test for asymmetry at the first fitting.

If the total difference exceeds 1/4 inch, you'll need to evaluate further (See Appendix 1).

TRACE OVER AND BALANCE THE MARKINGS

Remove both the Bodymap and the tracing paper from the table. Set the Bodymap aside and fold the tracing paper along the marked center front line so that it is folded in half. Pin the two sides together in several places and then secure the tracing paper to the table. On the side where you marked the bust radius, measure the distance between the bust point and the radius marking and record it in the Pattern Drafting Personal Measurement Chart.

Now you're going to "average" some of the markings for each side. (There's almost always a variance between them due to uneven pinning). Start, with a marker, by squaring a line from the CF fold at the highest levels of A (the front neck), B (the front draping point), C (the bust point), D (the underarm level, which may be above or below line C), E (the waistline/CF junction, disregarding any curve of the actual marked waistline), F (the approximate waist dart end point, below the waist level), and G- (the hem line) (See Fig. 3-19). Cut the paper along G. Label the lines accordingly.

Using a marker, average the CF to bust point distance by placing a dot on C halfway between the two marked bust points, if there's a difference. Disregard the level of the lower bust point, where applicable. From this averaged bust point position, draw a vertical line down to the hem line, making sure that it's parallel to the CF line (Fig. 3-20). This will be the waist dart centerline.

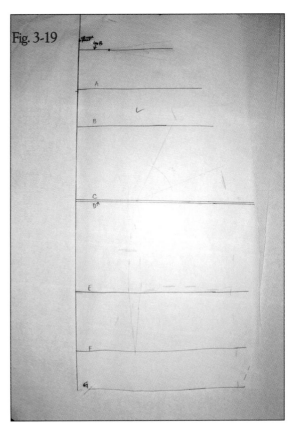

Fig. 3-19

Square a line from the CF fold at the highest levels of "A" (the front neck), "B" (the front draping point), "C" (the highest bust point), "D" (the highest underarm level), "E" (the waistline/CF junction), "F" (the waist dart end point), and "G" (the hem line).

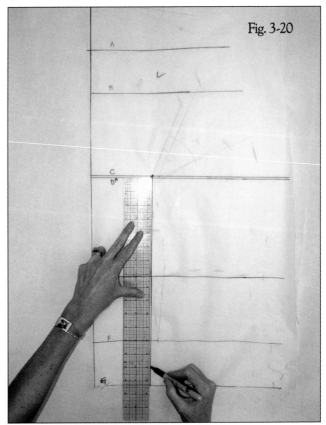

Fig. 3-20

Draw in the waist dart centerline from the averaged bust point position to the hem line.

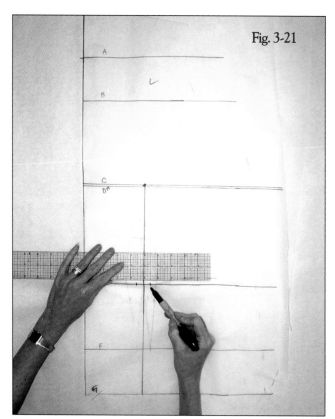

Fig. 3-21

The waist dart take-up is bisected by the center-line.

Then, move to the waist darts you penciled in earlier. If they're uneven, as they usually are, measure the dart take-up at both the waist (E) and below waist (F) levels on each side, add them together and divide by 2 to get the average dart take-up. Divide the dart take-ups at the waist and hip levels by 2 and place half of this amount on either side of the waist dart centerline at the corresponding levels (Fig. 3-21). For example, if the average dart take-up at the waist level is 1 inch, place a dot at 1/2 inch on either side of the waist dart centerline. If one side at the below waist level is 0 (the dart take-up at the dart tip is zero), and the other side is 1/2 inch, then the average is 1/4 inch at that level, so you would dot at 1/8 inch from each side of the centerline.

With a marker, draw in the waist dart by connecting the averaged waist level markings to the averaged hip level markings, converging on the waist dart centerline (Fig. 3-22). Next, connect the waist level markings to a point on the waist dart centerline that's 1 inch below the bust point.* Draw these darts with straight lines for now, although in finished garments they will sometimes be contoured or curved to better suit the roundness of the body.

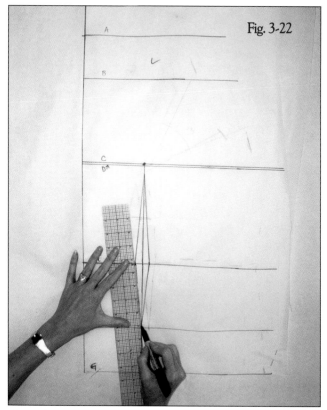

Fig. 3-22

Complete the dart legs using straight lines.

If you performed the protruding abdomen adjustment, average the width of the dart legs just under the bust point, and draw your dart legs from the waist to these points, rather than to 1 inch below the bust point. These waist dart legs are not bisected by the waist dart centerline, but rather the inside mark is on the waist dart centerline and the outside leg is to the outside of the waist dart centerline (towards the side seam) the amount of the averaged dart width, just as pinned.

Now you'll balance, or average, the side seams. Do this by placing an "X" halfway between the side seam markings on the upper layer of tracing paper and the side seam markings on the lower layer of tracing paper. With a pencil, draw in the corrected side seam by connecting the marks with a French curve and a straight edge, making sure that the side seam is vertical and parallel to the CF from the fullest part of the hip to the hem line.

Average the distance from the CF line of the front draping points, if there is a difference, and then refer to the dart angle comparison chart in order to proceed to the next step, drawing in the darts.*

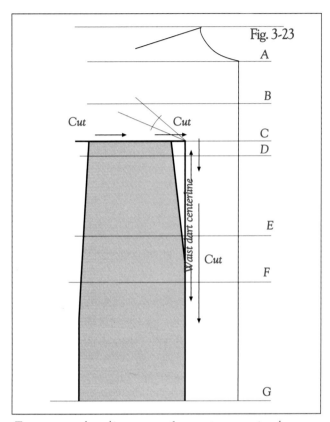

To correct the alignment of your pattern in the case of the protruding abdomen adjustment, cut the folded pattern from the side seam to the waist dart centerline at the bust point and then straight down to the hem line.

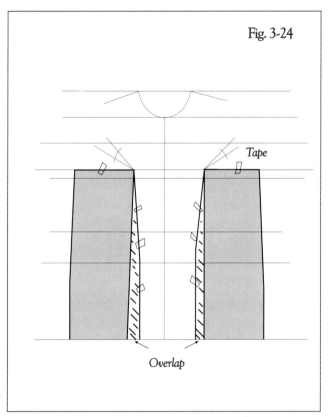

Re-tape the pattern pieces together, with the upper outside dart legs touching the bust points and the tracing paper overlapped between the bust points and hem lines.

**If you performed the protruding abdomen adjustment, you'll need to correct the alignment of your pattern before proceeding to the next step. To do this, cut the folded pattern along the bust point level line from the side seam to the waist dart centerline at the bust point. From here, cut down the waist dart's centerline all the way to the hem line (Fig. 3-23). Open out the front pattern and re-tape the pattern pieces together, with the upper outside dart legs touching the bust point and the tracing paper overlapped between the bust point and the hem line (Fig. 3-24). The waist dart centerline is parallel to the CF line and the hem lines are joined in one continuous horizontal line, despite the overlap.

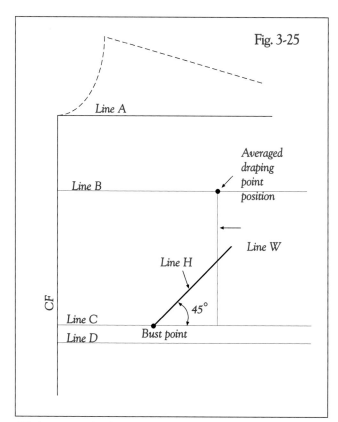

Fig. 3-25

Line A

Line B

Averaged
draping
point
position

Line W

Line H

45°

Line C

Line D

Bust point

CF

With a pencil, draw a line "H" from the bust point
towards the general area of the armhole. This line
should be at a 45-degree angle to line "C."

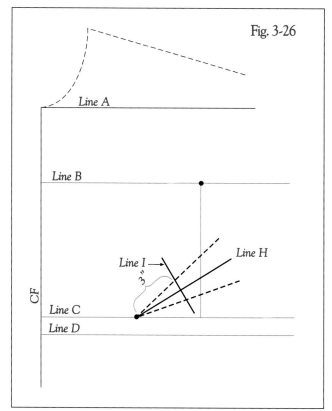

Fig. 3-26

Line A

Line B

Line I

Line H

3"

Line C

Line D

CF

Half of the bust dart angle goes on line "I" on
either side of line "H." Draw a dashed line through
these points.

DRAW IN THE CORRECTED FRONT DARTS

With a pencil, draw a line (H) from the bust point out towards the general area of the armhole that's at about a 45° angle to Line C (Fig. 3-25). Then, at 3 inches from the bust point on Line H, square a line (I). Divide the circled bust dart angle by 2, and place this amount on Line I on each side of H (Fig. 3-26). Then connect the bust point to the armhole with a dashed line going through each marked point on line I. Don't worry if the dart legs end up in a slanted position, too far up or too far down in the armhole, because this dart is temporary. Pin the dart closed along the dashed lines and, with a French curve, draw in a temporary armhole with a dashed line connecting the highest shoulder point, the front draping point, and the underarm level line (Fig. 3-27). On larger armholes, the French curve may need to be pivoted in order to draw in a smoothly-curved armhole. Because all garments require at least a small amount of ease in the armhole for movement, you'll now reduce the size of the bust dart slightly at the armhole. Open out the dart and mark a point on the temporary armhole 1/4 to 3/8 inch *inside* of each dart leg, with bust dart angles over 2 inches choosing the latter (Fig. 3-28). With a marker, redraw the bust dart, using these points on the armhole as the ends of the dart legs. Now measure the dart angle again (at the 3-inch point) and write the amount in the appropriate space in the Pattern Drafting Personal Measurement Chart. This is the bust dart angle, which will be used often in pattern drafting (Fig. 3-29).

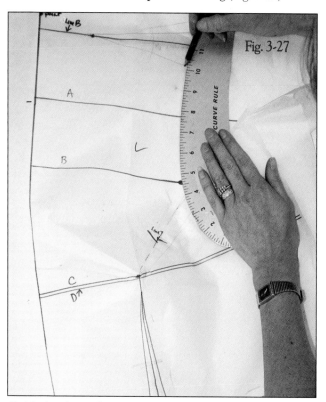

Fig. 3-27

Fold the dart closed along the dashed dart lines
and, with a French curve, draw in a temporary
armhole with a dashed line connecting the shoulder
point, the front draping point, and the underarm
level line.

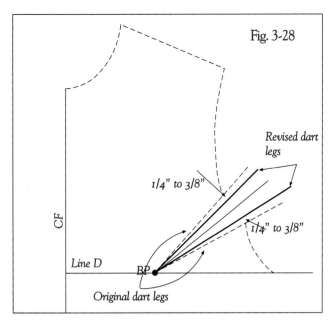

Fig. 3-28

Revised dart legs

1/4" to 3/8"

1/4" to 3/8"

CF

Line D

BP

Original dart legs

Reduce the size of the bust dart at the armhole by 1/4 inch to 3/8 inch on each leg.

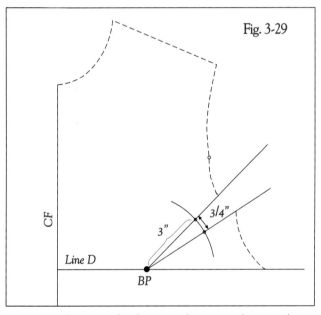

Fig. 3-29

CF

Line D

3"

3/4"

BP

Measure the straight distance between the two dart legs at 3 inches from the bust point. Write the amount in the Pattern Drafting Personal Measurement Chart.

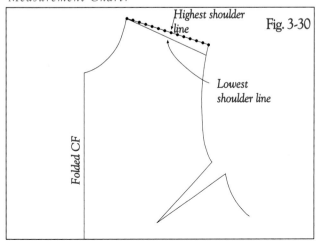

Highest shoulder line

Fig. 3-30

Lowest shoulder line

Folded CF

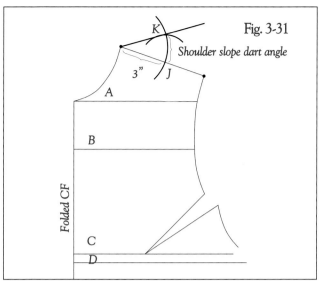

K

Fig. 3-31

Shoulder slope dart angle

3" J

A

B

Folded CF

C

D

Draw an arc at 3 inches from neck point which crosses the front shoulder line at "J." Set the compass so it equals the shoulder slope dart angle, its point on "J," and draw another arc which crosses the first at "K." Connect "K" to the neck point to form the back shoulder line.

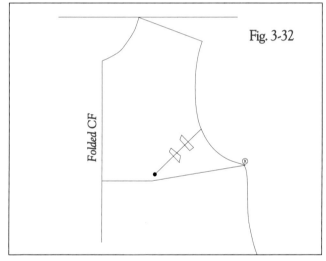

Fig. 3-32

Folded CF

⊗

After folding out the bust dart and drawing in the corrected armhole, mark the underarm point by marking an "X" inside a circle at the junction of the armhole and the side seam.

Trace over the front shoulder line, choosing the highest level, if there's a difference between them, on the upper and lower layers of tracing paper.

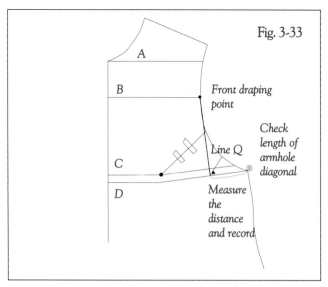

Fig. 3-33

A

B

Front draping
point

Check
length of
armhole
diagonal

Line Q

C

D

Measure
the
distance
and record

To mark the armhole width, square a line "Q" from the underarm level line "D" to the averaged front draping point. Measure this distance and record it in the angle formed by "Q" and "D." Check the armhole diagonal.

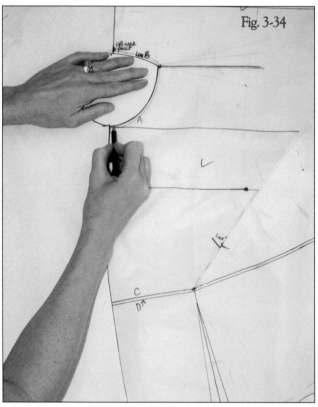

Fig. 3-34

Draw in the front and back neckline by placing the neck point of the neck template on the pattern's neck point and tracing around the template's curve until it touches the horizontal level of the center front and center back neck points.

COMPLETE THE FRONT PATTERN

With a marker, trace over the highest front shoulder line (if there's a difference between the two sides) (Fig. 3-30), and with a compass, redraw the 3-inch arc from the neck point, crossing the front shoulder line at J and extending the arc towards the center back line. Adjust the compass so it equals the shoulder slope dart angle circled above, and, placing the point of the compass at J, make a second arc which crosses the first at K. With a marker, connect the neck point to K, extending the line out a distance equal to the natural shoulder seam length (Fig. 3-31). This is the back shoulder line. Pin the two layers of tracing paper together a few times in the area of the bust dart, fold out the bust dart, and with a marker, redraw the armhole. The French curve should touch the underarm level, but may curve up before reaching the actual underarm point, and the armhole may appear to be smaller than you're used to seeing on patterns. Extend the side seam into the armhole area and mark an "X" inside a circle at this junction, the underarm point (Fig. 3-32). To mark the armhole width (the horizontal distance between the draping point and the underarm point), square a line (Q) from the underarm level line (D) to the averaged front draping point. Measure this distance and record it in the angle formed by Q and D (Fig. 3-33). Check that the armhole diagonal is between 3/4 inch and 1-1/8 inches long and adjust if necessary.

Connect the neck point with the front and back neck level markings by tracing around your neck template. Do this by aligning the neck points on the template with the neck points on the tracing paper and tracing around the template's curve until the curve turns into a horizontal line at the neck levels (Fig. 3-34). Raise or lower the template to meet the neck levels if you need to.

Untape or unpin the bust darts, turn the pattern over, and trace all of the corrected markings, including the back shoulder seam line, onto the other half of the tracing paper so that you'll have a corrected whole front pattern with the back shoulder lines included. Use a pencil when tracing the side seam marks, a marker on all the other marks.

COMPLETE THE BACK PATTERN

Separate the front pattern from the shoulder portion of the back pattern by cutting along Line B, the neck point level line. Set the front pattern aside and tape the back of the Bodymap to the table.

Tape the paper that has Line B and the back shoulder lines on it onto the Bodymap, with the CBs aligned and the CB neck point of the paper on top of the corrected CB neck position of the Bodymap (Fig. 3-35). (Either the edge of the gingham, if there was no variance, or the corrected distance towards the neck center, if there was.) Pin them together securely.

Tear off a piece of tracing paper larger than the back of the Bodymap, crease, and then draw a vertical line down its center, as you did for the front. Label this the Center Back (CB). Open it out and lay it over the back of the Bodymap with the CB lines aligned. Label the left and right sides.

With a pencil, trace over the corrected neck point positions, back shoulder seams lines, Line B, and the back neck-line (Fig. 3-36).

With either a flexible ruler or a measuring tape placed on its side, measure the length of the back neckline which you just traced. Refer to the back neck length measurement on the Pattern Drafting Personal Measurement Chart, and, if there's a difference, move the neck points in or, more likely, out horizontally and equally, one half the adjustment amount (a 5/8 inch maximum) per side (along Line B, not the back shoulder line), or until the pattern measurement equals the subject's. With a marker, connect the neck points to the CB neck using the neckline template as you did the front neck-line (Fig. 3-37).

From the corrected neck point, draw in a new shoulder seam line parallel to the old shoulder seam line and mark the endpoint at the correct shoulder seam length. Trace over the corrected shoulder seams and back neckline with a marker (Fig. 3-38).

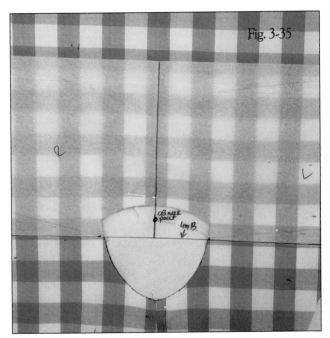

Fig. 3-35

Tape the paper containing line "B" on to the Bodymap with center backs aligned and the center back neck point of the paper on top of the corrected center back neck point of the Bodymap.

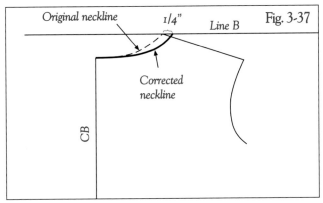

Fig. 3-37

To adjust the back neckline, move in or out on Line B, half the adjustment amount from each neck point. For example, if the personal measurement is 7, and the pattern measurement is 6-1/2, move out (to increase) 1/4 inch from each neck point along Line B. Draw in the corrected neckline.

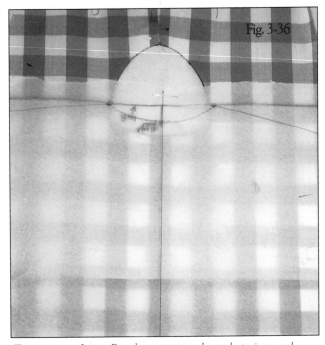

Fig. 3-36

Trace over Line B, the corrected neck points, the back shoulder lines, and the back necklines.

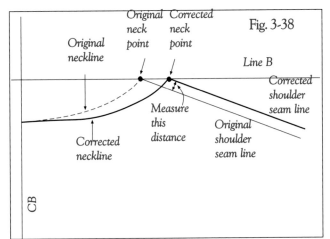

Fig. 3-38

From the corrected neck point, draw in a new shoulder seam line, parallel to the old shoulder seam line, and mark the end point at the correct shoulder seam length. Trace over the corrected shoulder seams and back neckline with a marker.

Now you're ready to trace over all of the markings on the back side of the Bodymap, just as you did the front. When you're done, remove the Bodymap from the table and fold the tracing paper in half along the center back line, pinning it together in a few places. With a marker, square a line from the CB at the highest level of the shoulder blade point (L), the back draping point (M), the waistline where it meets the CB (N), the waist dart end point below the waist (hip level) (O), and the hem line at the CB (G). Trace over the highest underarm level (P) with a pencil (Fig. 3-39).

Using a marker, average the CB to shoulder blade point distance by placing a dot on L halfway between the two marked shoulder blade points, if there's a difference. Disregard the level of the lower shoulder blade point.

From this averaged shoulder blade point position, draw a vertical line down to the hem line, making sure that it's parallel to the CB line. This is the waist dart centerline.*

Next, average the width of the lower part of the waist darts, the side seams, and the draping points as you did on the front, connecting the waist dart markings at waist level to the underarm level line, even if the subject's waist dart went higher when pinned. Average the width of the waist dart markings just below the underarm level if you performed the protruding buttocks adjustment. Extend the side seam into the armhole area, marking the underarm point with an "X" inside a circle. Draw in a temporary armhole by connecting the shoulder seam endpoint to this underarm point with a dashed line, leaving the dart unfolded. Cut the tracing paper across Line G, the hem level line. If you performed the protruding buttocks adjustment, you'll need to correct the alignment of your pattern before proceeding to the next step. To do this, cut the folded pattern from the side seam to the waist dart centerline. From here, cut down the waist dart's centerline all the way to the hem line. Open out the back pattern and re-tape the pattern pieces together, with the outside dart leg touching the top of the waist dart centerline and the tracing paper overlapped between the underarm level and the hem line. The waist dart centerline is parallel to the CB line and the hem lines are joined in one continuous horizontal line, despite the overlap (Fig. 3-40).

If you performed the protruding buttocks adjustment, correct the alignment of your pattern before proceeding to the next step.

*If the averaged shoulder blade point is close to the CB, the waist dart centerline will be in an awkward position. Move it out toward the side so it lies roughly halfway between the CB and the averaged back draping point. However, leave the averaged shoulder blade point in its original position.

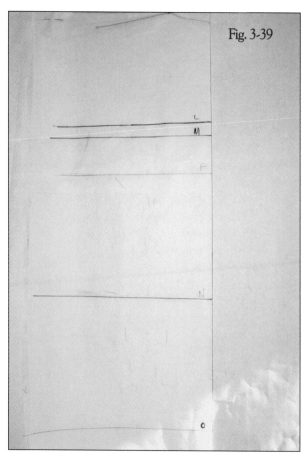

Fig. 3-39

With a marker, square a line from the center back at the level of the highest shoulder blade point ("L"), the back draping point ("M"), the waistline where it meets CB ("N"), the highest waist dart end point below the waist (hip level) ("L"), and the hem line ("G"). Trace over the highest underarm level ("P") with a pencil.

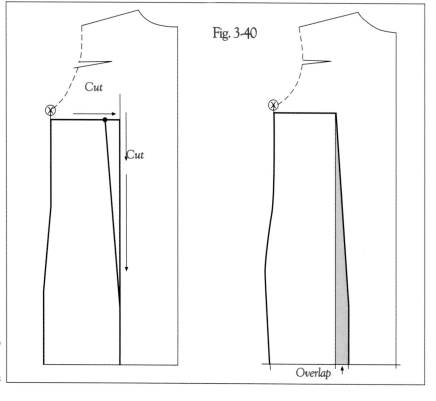

Fig. 3-40

From the averaged shoulder blade point, with a pencil, draw in the upper back dart by first drawing its center horizontally out to the armhole. Halve the angle and place each half on either side of the centerline at 3 inches away from the shoulder blade point, as you did on the front with the bust dart (Fig. 3-41). With a marker, reduce the back dart at the armhole by 1/4 inch on each dart leg. (If the corrected total dart is less than 1/4 inch at the armhole, you may delete it.)

Fold out and pin the upper back darts on the corrected dart legs and, with a pencil, draw in the back armholes, connecting the shoulder seam endpoint to the underarm point with a French curve, passing directly through or slightly to the outside of the back draping point. To mark the armhole width, square a line (R) from the underarm level line (P) to the averaged draping point. Measure this distance and record it in the angle formed by R and P (Fig. 3-42). Check that the armhole diagonal is between 1 and 1-1/2 inches and change it if necessary.

Untape or unpin the upper back darts, turn the pattern over, and trace all of the corrected markings onto the other half of the tracing paper, so that you'll have a corrected whole back pattern. Use a pencil when tracing the side seam marks, a marker on all of the other marks.

TRUE THE FRONT AND BACK PATTERNS

Double-check your pattern's length balance by superimposing the entire pattern over the entire Bodymap. Align the CB neck over the corrected CB neck position of the Bodymap, with the centerlines right on top of each other and the neck points of both the front and back patterns touching Line B, possibly at different places if the back neck width was changed. The waist and hem markings at CF and CB on both the Bodymap and the pattern should align. If they don't, check every pattern drafting step again to find your mistake. Keeping the pattern's CF and CB lines parallel, align the neck point and check that the shoulder slope dart angle is correct.

Fold the back and front patterns along their respective centerlines. Align the folded front and back patterns with hem levels even and grain lines parallel from hem to underarm level and the circled "X"s denoting the underarm points either touching, or along the same vertical line. (As long as the difference between the two underarm levels is less than 1/2 inch, disregard it; it may have been caused by a slightly slanted straight-edge when marked. If it's more, double-check the marks on the gingham. At this point, you may disregard the lower level, usually the back, but you may want to consider re-draping the upper portion of the Bodymap to check this, paying particular attention to the bust and upper back darts.) Disregard any overlapping of the waist and hip areas.

Extend the underarm level Line D from the front to the back with a marker.

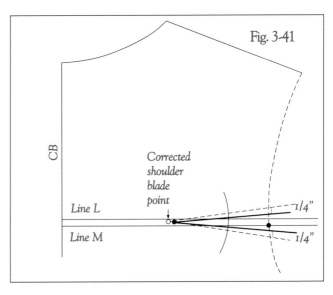

Reduce the upper back dart by a total of 1/2 inch at the armhole, as you did the bust dart.

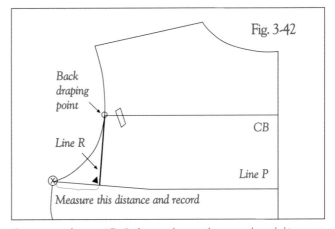

Square a line, "R," from the underarm level line, "P," to the averaged draping point. Measure this distance and record it in the angle formed by "R" and "P."

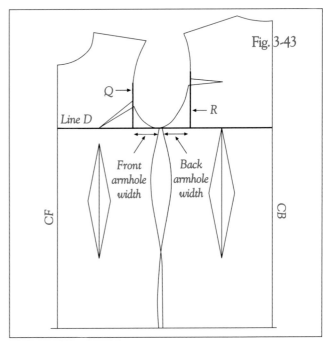

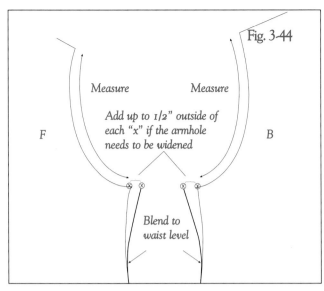

Check the armhole size and adjust at the side seams if necessary.

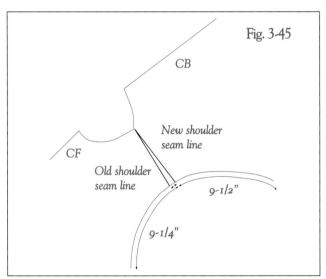

Move the shoulder line back or forward at the armhole in order to make the back armhole at least 1/4 inch longer than the front. Keep the neck point in the same position.

Extend the underarm level from the front pattern onto the back pattern with a marker, making the side seams the same length (Fig. 3-43). If there was a difference in the underarm levels, measure and add it to the armhole dart (either the bust or upper back dart) by making the dart bigger, reversing the techniques pictured in Figs. 3-28 and 3-41, using the difference as the reduction amount. Add the front and back armhole widths together, in order to check the total armhole width. The total armhole width equals 1/2 the measured bicep circumference minus 1/2 inch, on average. If yours is less than this, recheck that your averaged draping points and averaged side seam points were positioned correctly. If yours is more, proceed and check this at a fitting. To determine the proper side seam position, compare the separate armhole widths of the front and back patterns. The armhole width of the front should be 1/2 to 3/4 inch greater than the back, with bust sizes under 40 choosing the former. With a different-colored marker, trace over or redraw the corrected armholes. For example, if the front distance was 3 inches and the back was 3-1/2 inches, the front armhole width is 1/2 inch less than the back and it should be 1/2 inch more. Change them by moving the underarm points accordingly (horizontally in or out), adding the difference all the way down the side seam of the appropriate pattern and subtracting the difference all the way down the side seam of the other. In this example, move at least 1/2 inch into the front measurement, making it 3-1/2 inches and the back 3 inches.

With a flexible ruler or a measuring tape standing on its edge, measure the front and back armholes separately, darts folded out, then add the measurements together to get a total armhole length. Check to see if it's an appropriate size by adding 6 inches to the subject's bicep circumference (refer to the Pattern Drafting Personal Measurement Chart). The entire armhole should be equal to or greater than this total. If it's not, the armhole is too small and must be adjusted. If it's a small difference, less than 1 inch, add half the amount to each of the armholes by extending the underarm points out horizontally (Fig. 3-44). If it's a large difference, the preceding pattern drafting steps should be rechecked, especially those relating to the shoulder seam lines and dart angles, after ascertaining that the bicep circumference measurement was accurate. If you find no errors, extend the underarm points and check this during a fitting.

To determine the proper shoulder seam position, compare the measurements of the front and back armholes. In most cases, the back armhole is slightly (1/4 to 1/2 inch) longer than the front armhole. If this is not the case on your pattern, and your subject does not appear to have an over-erect posture (evidenced by a deleted upper back dart on the completed back pattern), tape the patterns together along the shoulder lines and redraw the shoulder line, adding to the back and subtracting from the front, so that the back armhole is 1/4 inch greater than the front armhole (Fig. 3-45). If your subject does have an over-erect posture, leave the shoulder line as is and check its position at the first garment fitting.

To average the side seam curve, align and pin the folded patterns so that the corrected underarm points are together and the CF and CB fold lines are parallel (Fig. 3-46). (In most cases, the folds will not be aligned right on top of each other.) Using a marker, average the side seam curve and cut along the corrected side seam from the hem to the armhole on all layers of paper.

Join the patterns together at the side seam/underarm point as if it were a garment to be sewn together, for the first few inches below the underarm point, and true the bottom of the underarm when necessary with a French curve (Fig. 3-47).

To create side seam cross marks at the waist level, align the front and back patterns with hem lines even and side seams touching at the narrowest part, overlapping the upper and lower parts of the pattern. Connect the CF waist point to the CB waist point with a straight line (Fig. 3-48). The points at which this straight line crosses each side seam are the waist level cross marks for joining the side seams.

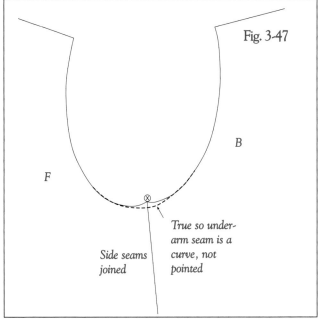

Join the patterns at the side seam/underarm point, as if they were going to be sewn together, and blend the curve.

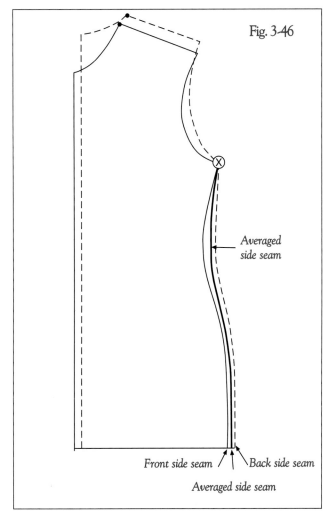

To average the side seam, align and pin the folded patterns together so that the underarm points are aligned and the centerlines are parallel. When the patterns are aligned with hem lines even, the front neck and waist points may be higher than, equal to, or lower than the back neck point depending on the individual.

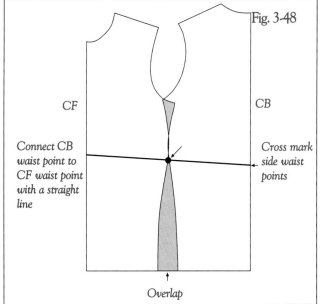

To create a side seam cross mark, align the patterns with hem levels even and side seams touching at the approximate waist level. Connect the center back waist point to the center front waist point with a straight line and cross mark the side waist points on each pattern.

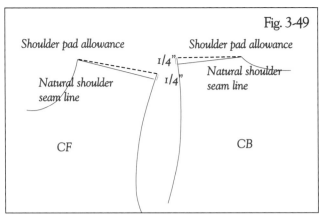

Fig. 3-49

Shoulder pad allowance

Shoulder pad allowance

1/4"
1/4"

Natural shoulder
seam line

Natural shoulder
seam line

CF

CB

Add 1/4 inch to the height of each shoulder tip to allow for a 1/2-inch thick shoulder pad.

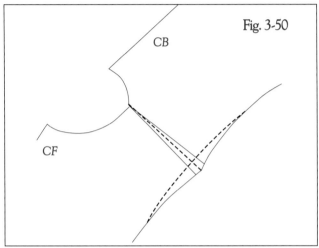

Fig. 3-50

CB

CF

Tape the pattern together at the raised shoulder seam lines and true the armhole by blending with a French curve, so the armhole does not have an angle at the shoulder seam line.

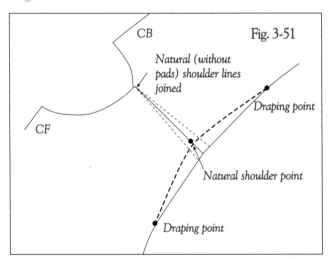

CB

Fig. 3-51

Natural (without
pads) shoulder lines
joined

Draping point

CF

Natural shoulder point

Draping point

Aligning the pattern pieces along the natural shoulder lines, draw in another armhole, blending it smoothly into the draping points and passing it through or near the natural shoulder points.

MARK THE GARMENT SHOULDER SEAM LENGTH, ADD A SHOULDER PAD ALLOWANCE, AND TRUE THE ARMHOLE

Referring to the Pattern Drafting Personal Measurement Chart, compare the natural shoulder seam length to the garment shoulder seam length. If there is a difference (as there usually is), extend the shoulder seam line out until it measures the garment shoulder seam length measurement, on both the front and the back. Next, add the shoulder pad allowance onto both as well, so that your Bodymap base pattern will have reference lines for both those garments which call for shoulder pads and those that don't. Most shoulder pads used in contemporary patterns are 1/2-inch thick, which is why you used this size when measuring the neck to bicep length and that's why you'll use it here. (If the subject has extremely sloped shoulders and/or wants a thicker pad, or you used another size to measure, use that figure instead.)

Raise each shoulder point half the height of the pad, in this case 1/4 inch, and taper to zero at the neck point (Fig. 3-49). Check the length of the shoulder seam lines and label the raised lines "shoulder pad allowance." Trim away the extra tracing paper along the new shoulder seam lines. Keep the patterns folded along the center front and center back and tape them together at the new shoulder seam lines, with the seams aligned from neck point to end point. Using a very shallow side of the French curve, true the armhole at the outside edge of the shoulder seam by blending from draping point to draping point, passing near or through the garment shoulder seam endpoint, so the armhole becomes a smoothly blended curve for its entire length (Fig. 3-50). The amount of curve at the shoulder junction is affected not only by the squareness of the shoulders, but also by the length of the shoulder seam. In some cases, the armhole will be almost a straight line at this junction, perpendicular to the shoulder seam; in others, it will be more curved. Truing the armhole may lengthen or shorten the shoulder seam by a small amount, and you may have to pass slightly outside of the draping points to make a smooth transition. Aligning the pattern pieces along the natural (without shoulder pad allowance) shoulder lines, draw in another armhole, blending it smoothly into or very closely outside of the draping points, and passing through or near the natural shoulder point (Fig. 3-51). This natural armhole will be used for some of the sleeveless garments.

True the neckline at the neck points, making sure you don't narrow the neck as you do it (Fig. 3-52). Cut the extra tracing paper from the neck and outermost armhole.

Measure the final shoulder seam lengths from the neck point to both the natural and garment endpoints, and, if they've changed, change them in the pattern drafting personal measurement chart.

TRANSFER THE BUST AND UPPER BACK DARTS TO THEIR PROPER POSITIONS

If there is no asymmetry adjustment to be made, you can separate the right and left sides of the patterns to facilitate the dart manipulation process. If there is, perform the dart transferring processes on each side and plan to draft each pattern separately for the right and left sides. See Fig. 3-53 and Appendix 2 (page 116) for instructions on performing the asymmetry adjustment. If you performed the protruding abdomen or buttocks adjustments, adjust your pattern first by referring to "Correcting the Pattern for Protruding Abdomen or Buttocks" on page 59.

On the front pattern, draw a straight line from the bust point to a point on the side seam that's 2 inches below the underarm point. Cut along this line and then along the lower leg of the existing bust dart, to, but not through, the bust point, leaving about 1/8 inch of paper still attached (Fig. 3-54). Close the existing dart by bringing the cut lower leg up to meet the upper leg and tape it down securely in this position. The opening that occurred in the side seam is the new bust dart, and the cut edges of the tracing paper are the new dart legs. Tape a strip of tracing paper under the opening and draw in the dart centerline by connecting the bust point to the point on the side seam that's halfway between the new dart legs. Draw in the garment dart tip 3/4 to 1 inch away from the bust point on the dart centerline. Draw straight lines connecting the new dart legs to the garment dart tip and to the bust

Draw a straight line from the bust point to a point on the side seam that's 2 inches below the underarm point. Cut along this line and then along the lower leg of the original bust dart, to, but not through, the bust point.

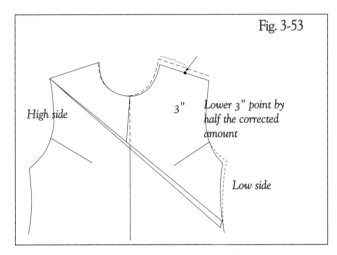

True the neckline at the neck points, making sure you don't narrow the neck as you do it.

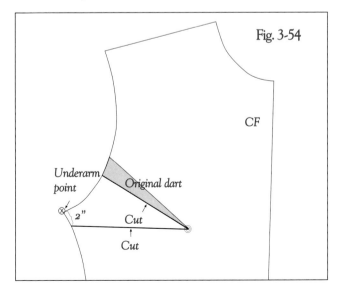

To make an asymmetry adjustment, draw a line from the shoulder tip of the higher shoulder to the side seam of the opposite side. Cut from the low side along this line, to, but not through, the shoulder tip and lower the 3-inch point one half the adjustment amount. True the side seam and centerline and repeat on the back.

point (Fig. 3-55). Fold out the new dart, to correct the dart underlay, and re-draw and trim the side seam.

Because the upper back dart really shapes the entire area, rather than just the shoulder blade, and the back apex position is so variable, the upper back darts are in a pretty standard position, although the dart take-up and length (which can be fine-tuned at a fitting) will vary from person to person. On the back pattern, find the midpoint of the shoulder seam and square a line from it into the shoulder blade area. Mark a point

on this line 4 to 4-1/2 inches from the shoulder seam line (the smaller distance for dart angles under 1/2 inch). Cut along the lower leg of the existing dart to its tip, then up to the tip of the new dart (Fig. 3-56). Close the old dart and draw the new dart, moving its tip 1 inch closer to the shoulder seam line. True the armhole by connecting the shoulder point to the original lower dart leg/armhole junction (the widest armhole mark at this point) and on to the underarm level line as before (Fig. 3-57). Fold out the new dart and redraw the shoulder

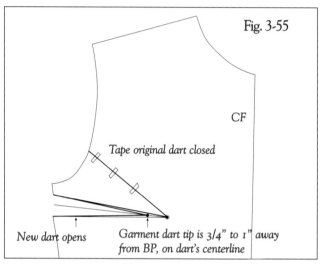

Close the existing dart by bringing the cut lower leg up to meet the upper let and tape it down securely in this position. Draw in the new garment dart.

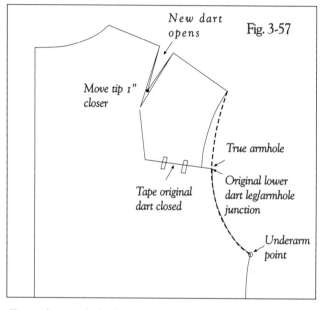

True the armhole by connecting the shoulder point to the original lower dart leg/armhole junction and connect this point to the underarm point.

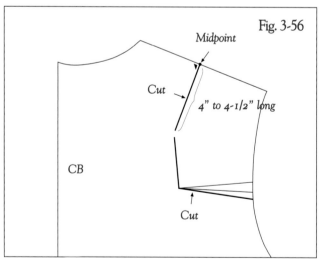

Cut along the lower leg of the original dart to its tip then up, to, but not through, the tip of the new dart. Close the old dart.

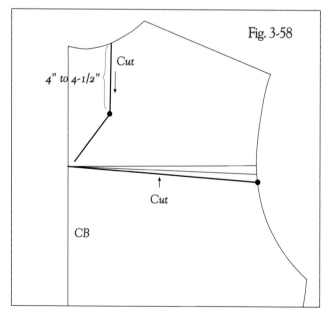

For a dowager's hump, cut along the lower dart leg of the original dart, to, but not through, the center back (or to the apex of the upper back curve). Cut from the neckline to the new dart tip, then diagonally to the same point on the center back.

seam line.

For a dowager's hump, where the upper dart was pinned out all the way to or almost to the CB, transfer the dart to the neckline. To do this, draw a 4 to 4-1/2 inch line that's parallel to and 2 inches from the CB line. Cut along this line and then diagonally to the CB line at the level of the original dart (Fig. 3-58). Close the original dart, patch the opening with tracing paper, and draw in the neck dart with its tip at 3 to 3-1/2 inches below the neckline. Disregard the small opening on the diagonal line (Fig. 3-59). Fold out the neck dart and true the neckline by connecting the CB neck point to the neck level of the *outside* dart leg (Fig. 3-60). True the armhole.

Copy the Bodymap onto a clean piece of pattern paper, adding ease on each side seam, from underarm point to hem line.

To do this, widen the underarm points horizontally 3/4 inch, the side waist points 1/4 inch, and the hip 1/2 inch. Connect these new side seam points with a French curve, making sure the side seam is squared with the hem line from the fullest part of the hip down. Repeat on the back and true the armhole at the underarm points as you previously did (refer to page 54). Measure and record the final front and back armhole lengths in the Pattern Drafting Personal Measurement Chart.

You may be tempted to test your base pattern in muslin now, but don't yet, because this garment was drafted for use with a sleeve, which you will draft next. When you finish with the basic sleeve, it's advisable to make the base pattern up in muslin to check that the bust point, shoulder seams, and side seams are in their proper positions, that the shaping in each of the darted areas is correct, and that the hem line is level and parallel to the floor on all sides. Once this fine-tuning is performed, your drafted patterns will not need a muslin testing, except in the case of contoured garments.

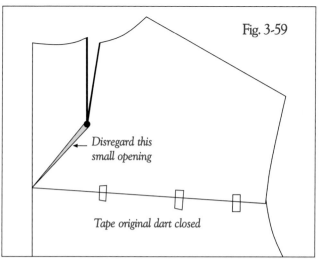

Fig. 3-59

Disregard this small opening

Tape original dart closed

Tape the original dart closed and draw in the new dart.

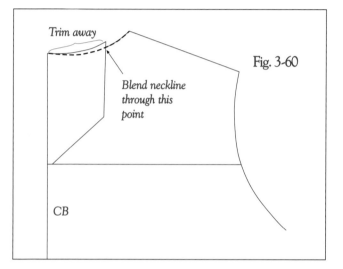

Trim away

Fig. 3-60

Blend neckline through this point

CB

Fold out the neck dart and true the neckline by connecting the center back neck point to the neck level of the outside dart leg.

CORRECTING THE PATTERN FOR PROTRUDING ABDOMEN OR BUTTOCKS

If you performed either of the protruding adjustments, you'll need to change your pattern to a princess line pattern in order to keep your cross grain lines level at the hem line in a finished garment. To do this, for a protruding abdomen adjustment, first mark the bust point onto the side section at the outside dart leg (which is right on top of the averaged bust point) (Fig. 3-61A). Find the midpoint of the armhole and, with a French curve, draw and cut a curved line to the bust point. Cross mark this line 1-1/2 inches above the bust point and cross mark the two waist dart legs 1-1/2 inches below the bust point. Untape the overlapped waist dart and separate the pattern pieces (Fig. 3-61B). Close the original bust dart (Fig. 3-61C). Add ease to the side panel's bust area by cutting from the bust point to the side seam and spreading the pattern 1/4 inch at the bust point. Patch this opening and blend the side

panel at the bust point, marking "ease" between the cross marks (Fig. 3-61D). Mark the grain line on the side panel perpendicular to the hem line. Untape the overlapped portion and return the side panel to its original position by aligning all cut edges as they were.

For the protruding buttocks adjustment, follow the same process on the back of the pattern, drawing the curved line from just below the upper back dart. On the back, transfer the upper back dart to the princess style line, as described in Chapter 4 (page 81, Steps 6, 7, and 8), or move it to the neckline if the subject had a dowager's hump. Do not add additional ease in the back side panel as is described for the front.

To perform the asymmetry adjustment, tape your pattern to a large piece of tracing paper, with the hem line continuous and the waist dart centerlines touching at the hem line. Refer to Fig. 53 to perform the adjustment. Make sure to true all seam and centerlines.

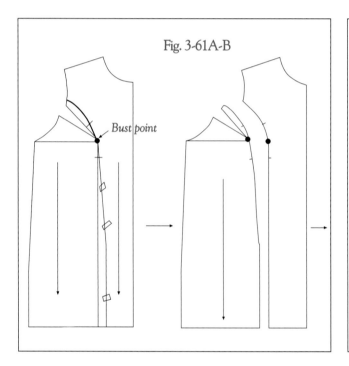

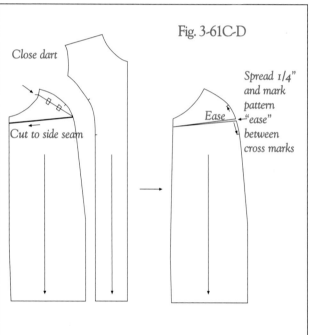

If you performed a protruding abdomen adjustment, change the front pattern to a princess line pattern.

CREATE THE SLEEVE PATTERN

Drafting a basic sleeve to fit your Bodymap requires that certain measurements be taken on your completed Bodymap pattern. First, measure the Shoulder Point to Underarm Levels on both the front and back of your Bodymap at the tip of the shoulder pad addition and from the outside (garment) shoulder point (Fig. 3-62). Add them together and divide this sum by 2, then subtract 1 inch. This is your approximate cap height. Now, double-check this figure by comparing it to the cap height you determined previously, when the garment shoulder seam length was measured (with the shoulder pad). These two figures should be within an inch of each other. If not, recheck all measurements. If nothing changes, continue on, but test the first garment in muslin.

You will draft the sleeve for a shoulder-padded garment. To draft a separate sleeve using the natural shoulder seam length (for use without shoulder pads), reduce the cap height by subtracting the shoulder pad height, plus 1/2 inch. This sleeve may not have enough cap height to fall properly as a set-in sleeve, so you should only use it when this is not a factor. Incidentally, you may add a little buckram or other stiffener to the bottom of your shoulder pads in order to prevent them from folding over at the shoulder point when the garment shoulder seam extends past the shoulder bone, and the shape of the shoulder pad's other edge should be trimmed to match the shape of the armhole where it will lie.

After drafting your basic sleeve, you may choose to draft a "shirt" sleeve following the same steps below but using a cap height of 4 to 5 inches.

You will use the higher of the two cap heights as the starting point for your draft. You'll also need the following measurements from your Pattern Drafting Personal Measurement Chart:

A. Front armhole length
B. Back armhole length
C. Bicep circumference
D. Bicep to elbow
G. Back arm length
H. Front arm length

Tape your pattern paper (preferably gridded), approximately 30 x 30 inches, down to your table and draw a horizontal line across the paper at about 9 inches from the top. This is the bicep line.

First you'll draft the sleeve cap, which is the portion of the sleeve that lies above the underarm point level. From the approximate midpoint of the bicep guide line, draw a perpendicular line up towards the top of the paper, the length of which is your cap height. Mark this cap point with a dot. From this point, draw a diagonal line to the right (front) side of the bicep line, the length of which is equal to the front armhole measurement plus 1/4 inch. Draw a diagonal line on the left (back) as well, the length equal to the back armhole (Fig. 3-

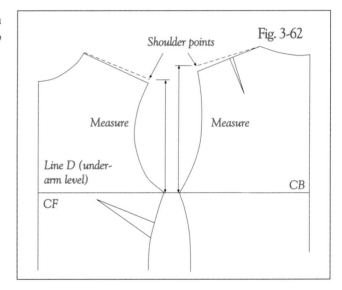

Fig. 3-62

Measure the shoulder point to the underarm level distance on both the front and back. Add them together, divide by 2, and subtract 1 inch. For example, if the front was 8 inches and the back 9 inches, 8 plus 9 equals 17, 17 divided by 2 equals 8-1/2 , 8-1/2 minus 1 equals 7-1/2. So, the desired cap height is 7-1/2 inches.

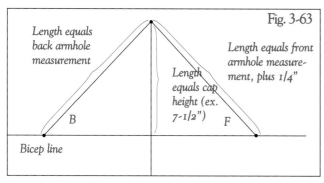

Fig. 3-63

Length equals back armhole measurement

Length equals front armhole measurement, plus 1/4

Length equals cap height (ex. 7-1/2")

B

F

Bicep line

From the cap point, draw a diagonal line to the right side of the bicep line, the length of which is equal to the front armhole measurement plus 1/4 inch. Draw a diagonal line on the left equal to the back armhole measurement.

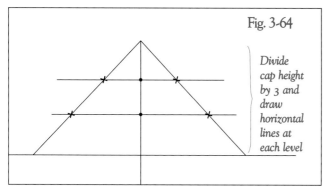

Fig. 3-64

Divide cap height by 3 and draw horizontal lines at each level

Place an "X" at the intersections of the diagonal lines and the horizontal lines.

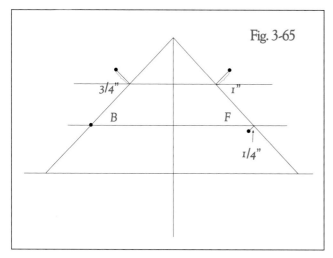

Fig. 3-65

3/4"   1"

B   F

1/4"

At each point where the two horizontal lines intersect the two diagonal lines, mark an "X." From the front lower "X" mark move inside the diagonal line 1/4 inch and put a dot here. On the upper "X" marks, move outside of the diagonals 1 inch on the front and 3/4 inch on the back. These dot positions are somewhat variable.

63). Measure the bicep line between these two points and compare it to the personal bicep measurement. It should be at least 2 inches greater. If it's not, and it sometimes isn't at this stage, you must extend the bicep line until it is 2 inches greater. Then re-draw the diagonal lines at a lower cap height point, which may take several attempts to get the armhole measurements to meet at the same point. At this point, the reduction in cap height has affected your perfect sleeve hang, and you have several options to consider. You can extend the underarm points of the bodice pattern out (equally on front and back) horizontally to make the armhole larger (tapered to the waistline), then return the cap height to its optimum position, you can extend the garment shoulder seam length the amount of the difference and leave the cap height as it is (lowering the underarm point slightly if the armhole measurement changes), or you can decide to do neither and accept the sleeve as it is . The second option is the best.

Once you've decided on the cap height, divide it by 3 and draw a horizontal line at this distance above the bicep line and one at this distance below the cap height point. At each point where the two horizontal lines intersect the two diagonal lines, mark an "X" (Fig. 3-64). From the front lower "X" mark, move inside the diagonal line, perpendicularly, 1/4 inch, and put a dot here. On the upper "X" marks, move outside of the diagonals, perpendicularly, 1 inch on the front and 3/4 inch on the back and dot (Fig. 3-65). (Reverse these measurements if the front armhole length is longer than the back, as seen in over-erect postures.) Connect the points on the top two-thirds of each side of the cap by aligning the French curve with all three points: the cap height point, the upper and lower dots on the front, and the upper dot and lower "X" mark on the back, extending the curve about 1/2 inch lower than the lower dots (Fig. 3-66). Do the front and then the back.

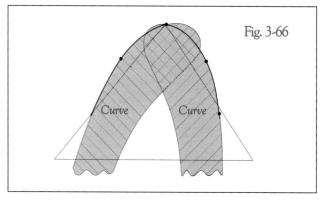

Fig. 3-66

Curve   Curve

Connect the points on the top two thirds of the cap by aligning the French curve with all three points (the cap point and the front two dots, the cap point and the back dot, and lower X).

Place the Bodymap back pattern right side down, on top of your sleeve draft, with underarm points touching, and pivot the back pattern up until its armhole touches the lowest point of the drawn curve. Trace the Bodymap's armhole curve onto the sleeve draft. Double cross mark both pattern pieces, then remove the Bodymap and blend the curve smoothly (Fig. 3-67). Do the same on the front, using the Bodymap front pattern. Move the cap point forward (towards the sleeve front) 5/8 inch.

Now you will draft the sleeve body. To determine the sleeve length, average the Front and Back Arm measurements by adding them together and dividing by 2. Add 1/2 inch to this measurement. Fold the pattern in half vertically, with underarm points touching and the bicep line aligned on top of itself. Tape the folded pattern down and draw the underarm seam line by squaring a line down from the bicep line/underarm point junction to the measurement of the sleeve length (Fig. 3-68). Draw the hem line at this level, making sure it's perpendicular to the fold. Cut the extra paper away from the pattern's hem and underarm seam lines, then open it out and trim the cap area as well. Refold the pattern in half, then in half again, finger pressing the creases, so that the bicep line is one fourth its size on the whole pattern. Open out the pattern and draw in the crease lines. Referring to the subject's bicep to elbow measurement, subtract 1/2 inch and draw in the elbow line at this distance below the bicep line, and label the center fold line "sleeve centerline" (Fig. 3-69). The sleeve cap may be eased into the armhole along its entire length except for the lower half of the front which is never eased, but sewn in a 1:1 ratio to the armhole. The majority of the ease will be in the top half of the cap. This is the straight

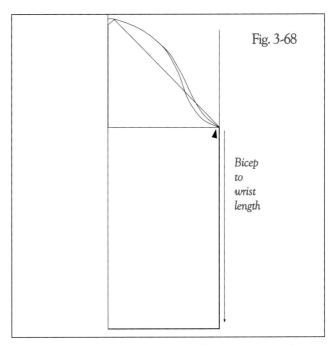

Fig. 3-68

Bicep to wrist length

Fold the pattern in half vertically with the underarm point touching and the bicep line on top of itself. Square a line from the bicep line/underarm point junction to the measurement of the sleeve length.

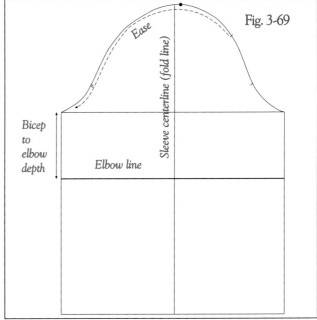

Fig. 3-69

Ease

Bicep to elbow depth

Sleeve centerline (fold line)

Elbow line

Mark the elbow line and the sleeve centerline.

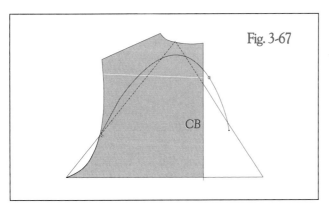

Fig. 3-67

CB

Place the Bodymap back pattern on the sleeve pattern, with underarm points touching, and pivot the Bodymap pattern until its armhole touches the lowest point of the sleeve curve. Trace the Bodymap's curve onto the sleeve draft and cross mark both pattern pieces.

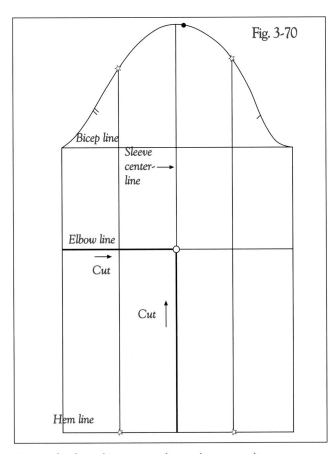

Fig. 3-70

Bicep line

Sleeve center-line →

Elbow line →

Cut

Cut ↑

Hem line

From the hem line, cut along the centerline, to, but not through, the elbow line, and from the back underarm seam, cut along the elbow line, to, but not through, the centerline.

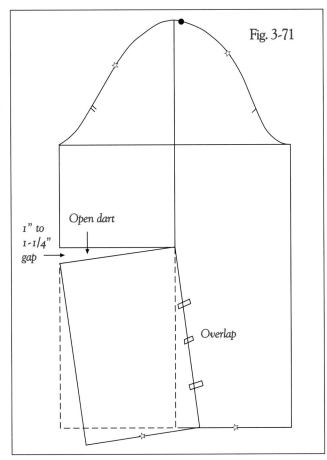

Fig. 3-71

1" to 1-1/4" gap →

Open dart ↓

Overlap

sleeve block, which will be used as a basis for other sleeve patterns, the first of which, the shaped sleeve, you'll draft now.

Make a tracing of the straight sleeve block, including the crease lines that divide the pattern into fourths, and set it aside. From the hem line, cut along the centerline to, but not through, the elbow line. From the back underarm seam, cut along the elbow line to, but not through, the centerline (Fig. 3-70). Pivot the cut pattern section towards the front until a 1- to 1-1/4-inch gap opens at the temporary back underarm seam line (Fig. 3-71). Tape the overlapping pattern sections together and add a tracing paper strip to the underside of the gap. Measure the hem line and divide it in two to find its center. Connect this point to the centerline at the elbow level. Draw in the elbow dart by connecting each point of the 1-inch opening at the back underarm seam to a point 3 inches towards the sleeve center, located on the elbow line (Fig. 3-72). If you wish, taper the wrist by narrowing the hem line by 1-1/2 inches on each side and connect these points to the corresponding underarm point. Fold out the elbow dart and re-draw the back underarm seam line. Open out the pattern and blend the hem line with a very gentle curve.

Now that your Bodymap Base Pattern is complete, you can draft just about any pattern you wish.

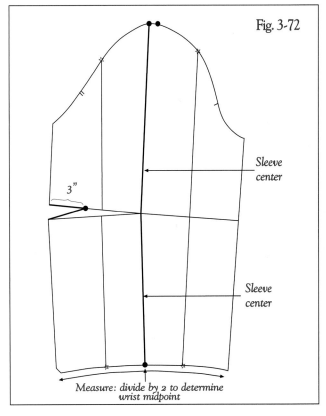

Fig. 3-72

Sleeve center

3"

Sleeve center

Measure: divide by 2 to determine wrist midpoint

LEFT: Pivot the bottom of the cut pattern section towards the front until a 1-inch gap appears on the back seam line.

ABOVE: Find the midpoint of the wrist and connect it to the elbow line/centerline junction. This is the sleeve centerline below the elbow.

CHAPTER 4

PATTERN DRAFTING: TOPS, JACKETS, AND DRESSES

There are three primary methods of creating clothing patterns: draping, flat pattern manipulation, and drafting. Draping is a process that creates patterns by molding a piece of fabric on a three-dimensional form—either on a dress form or on a real body. Flat pattern manipulation consists of transforming a base pattern into a fashion pattern by manipulation and/or contouring. Drafting is done by plotting and connecting points on paper which relate to certain body measurements and to the style of the desired garment. The Bodymapping process includes a combination of the three methods: draping the base pattern, flat pattern manipulating, and drafting fifteen basic "blocks," which are master patterns derived from the sloper to be used as the basis for fashion patterns.

The first three blocks you'll create are interim blocks—that is, they will be used as references or predecessors for some of the others. These include the:

CONTOUR BLOCK, for use with lowered necklines and sleeveless garments
KNIT BLOCK, for use with knits or fabrics that "grow"
EQUALIZED ARMHOLE BLOCK, in which the armholes have been made the same size in preparation for the drafting of garments with over-arm seams

The others, all of which can be lengthened into dresses or shortened into tops or jackets, can be used as they are, or they can be embellished with whatever details you like, such as collars, sleeve treatments, or neckline variations. Most importantly, the drafting of these blocks incorporates many important pattern drafting principles which will help "round out" your understanding of clothing design. The blocks include:

Two manipulated bust dart blocks:

FRENCH DART BLOCK, where the bust dart originates from the side waist point
NECK POINT DART BLOCK, where the bust dart originates from the neck point

Four style line blocks, where the garment shaping has been retained, but not as sewn triangular darts:

SHOULDER PRINCESS LINE BLOCK, where the style line that contains the bust and upper back shaping originates at the shoulder
ARMHOLE PRINCESS LINE BLOCK, where the style line that contains the bust and upper back shaping originates from the armhole
PANEL STYLE LINE BLOCK, where the style line does not contain the garment shaping but there is no sewn triangular bust dart
YOKE STYLE LINE BLOCK, where the front part of the yoke does not contain the bust dart shaping, but there are pleats below it which do; the back of the yoke can contain or release the upper back shaping

Three combination blocks, where the sleeve and bodice are combined in various ways that differ from the base pattern:

KIMONO BLOCK, where the sleeve and bodice are combined
RAGLAN-SLEEVED BLOCK, where part of the shoulder and armhole of the bodice become part of the sleeve
MOCK-DROPPED SHOULDER BLOCK, based on the kimono block but with a separate sleeve and a slightly shaped armhole

And three sleeveless blocks, which demonstrate the use of pattern-making principles like contouring, dart releasing, and added fullness:

TANK TOP BLOCK, which has a contoured neckline and armhole
CAP-SLEEVED BLOCK, which has part of the garment shaping released into the armhole
CAMISOLE BLOCK, which has a contoured neckline and shoulder straps

You'll find a gallery of other pattern-making details included, such as adding collars, overlaps, and facings, creating sleeve variations, and adding fullness and flare. And finally, you'll learn how to use these blocks in conjunction with commercial sewing patterns, in order to add the detail you want to an already fit-perfected sewing pattern (See Appendix 3).

Once you have a library of these basic blocks, you can use them to design just about any garment you wish. And because they're based on your perfectly-fitted sloper, the new designs will always fit, with only a minimum of fine-tuning. But before you get started, give some thought to what your designing goals are. In order to design productively, you must have a specific "fit" in mind for each type of garment—you must have already determined the garment lengths and widths you'll be most satisfied with. Lengths are pretty easy; just look in your closet to get an idea of what you're comfortable with. But deciding on widths takes a bit more evaluation.

How much extra fabric do you need over and above the circumference of your body measurement? This is a good question, one that only you can answer. Your initial Bodymap was draped without much ease at all. Then, in the final pattern drafting process, ease was added to each side seam, for a total of 3 inches of ease at the bust, slightly less at the hip. Three inches of ease is considered the minimum amount in a fitted garment, but how much more do you need? How much is too much? Again, only you can decide. Keep in mind that commercial patterns for the home sewer, as well as for the ready-to-wear industry, are intended for mass markets—the more people they can fit, the more they will sell. How do they fit the largest amount of people? By making the patterns loose-fitting and often shapeless. Remember, only a small percentage of pattern consumers will actually have a sloper that is identical to the pattern company's, so by the addition of extra ease, patterns can be worn by more people. But when you start your drafting with a perfectly-fitted sloper, you can get away with much less ease than you may think—a well-designed, close-fitting dress is just as comfortable as a looser fitting garment when you're not constantly struggling with it or rearranging its parts, because fit and comfort are synonymous.

You will also need to consider that the blocks are designed to, whenever possible, maintain the integrity of the grain-controlling darts. The popularity of oversized and loose-fitting garments presents a real problem when you're trying to keep the grain-controlling darts in charge of the garment: when there's a lot of extra room in the circumference of the garment as compared to the circumference of the body, the garment can shift around as the body moves, and therefore, the bust dart, in its many forms, can become displaced and provide shape for a curve that's actually inches away. This is apparent when the garment is a jacket or a shirt that's left open and is particularly obvious when the garment has been fitted to a large bust. Additionally, ease should be somewhat relative in a garment; too little ease in one area may not combine well

with a lot of ease in another area. For this reason, as well as to make the garment more comfortable, pattern designers often decrease or eliminate the bust dart in this type of garment, usually by moving it into the armhole and leaving it left unsewn. As you learned by performing the Bodymapping process, the properly-sized bust dart controls not only the shape of the garment's bust area, but also the change in length from the center of the garment front to the side. Therefore, by decreasing its size, there is excess length on the side of the garment, which manifests itself differently depending on the fluidity of the fabric. Stiffer fabrics tend to have a diagonal fold going from the bust point to the armhole, while drapey fabrics may have a combination of this fold and a sagging side seam, which makes the center front of the garment seem to "ride up." Proper under-structure in a tailored garment will eliminate some, but not all, of this excess, but most other tops will droop or fold in some way. Rather than simply adding an unattractively long side seam dart, or deleting the bust shaping altogether, I've tried to incorporate the darts in creative ways which limit bust dart displacement, while still allowing the garment to be made as loose as desired. In addition, I've included a few ideas for adding extra ease in fitted garments, so that you have the ease and move-ability you need in a garment which complements your figure rather than simply covers it like a sack.

Many of the garments pictured in this book have the waist shaping diminished or deleted. This can be done by straightening the side seams—connecting the underarm point to the full hip point and continuing down to the hem line—and crossing out the waist darts. This technique usually results in a slightly bias side seam, one that gets wider at the hem line for a fuller hip, or narrower at the hem line for a narrower hip, although this second scenario is less common (Fig. 4-1). When side seams are diagonal, that part of the hem line, when trued, becomes slightly bias as well. A better alternative is to square the side seam to the hem line at the widest point (usually the hip as opposed to the underarm point), thereby attaining a side seam on the lengthwise grain. (A vertical side seam is less likely to stretch and dip than a diagonal one.) Doing so not only deletes the side waist shaping, it also adds additional ease in the underarm area (assuming the hips are wider than the underarm points) (Fig. 4-2). If this is acceptable to you, make sure that whatever change is made to the front bodice is also made to the back bodice, and that armholes of the sleeve are widened exactly as much as the armholes of the bodice have been. (You can taper to the existing sleeve wrist line.) Widening the side seams too much, however, can ultimately cause the side seams to droop as well, so it's a balancing act.

For fitted garments where the waist shaping has been retained, the guidelines that I have used most successfully are: Add an additional 1/4 inch in width to each side seam of the basic block (including the sleeve). This gives a bit more than 4 inches of ease around the bust, waist, and hips. For many people, this will be plenty, and some of this may even be pinned out at a fitting, but at least it's there should you need it. Adding additional ease to the side seams may also result in the need to adjust the waist darts, by lengthening them, dividing them, or reducing their take-up, which is easily done at a fitting. Incidentally, the set-in sleeved garment is, by the nature of the armhole and sleeve shape, the least comfortable garment you can make. Consider this when designing your garments. Try to pair a set-in sleeve with a bodice that has no waist dart shaping, or an open front like the "Messini" and "Salonika" jackets pictured on page 76. Add an inverted center back pleat on a set-in sleeved design, or broaden the pattern slightly across the upper back. Shallow out the lower armhole curves of the back armhole (by increasing the length of the armhole diagonal) and the sleeve to give you more forward reach. Use a two-part set-in sleeve, which has extra ease added in the bicep area. Design your waist-fitted garments with kimono sleeves for added comfort. As you can see, there are many choices to be made in the balancing of a garment's look, fit, and comfort, but they're choices you can make according to your own set of priorities.

As in the teaching of most crafts, there are many means to the same end in the instruction of pattern drafting; completely different steps from various teachers and textbooks result in essentially the same end result. I've studied and tested a variety of methods and have chosen the techniques used here for very specific reasons, certainly because they require a minimal amount of calculation and are achieved with few steps. But most importantly, I have favored the technique of "slash and spread" dart manipulation, although it's a bit messy, because from a learning standpoint, the pattern changes are far more understandable, and you're likely to grasp relationships more quickly than you will from plotting points on paper. A warning, however: Don't combine steps you've learned from other resources with the steps explained here unless you have considerable pattern drafting experience. This reference is intended to be a start-to-finish process, and while you may think you're just making some innocent changes, you could be making a costly mistake. If you absolutely must make a change that is not covered here, it is wise to make a muslin test garment before cutting into a finer piece of cloth.

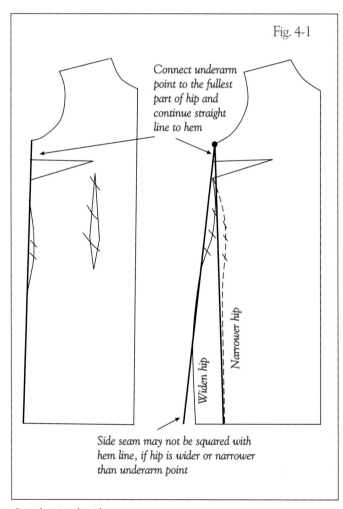

Straightening the side seam

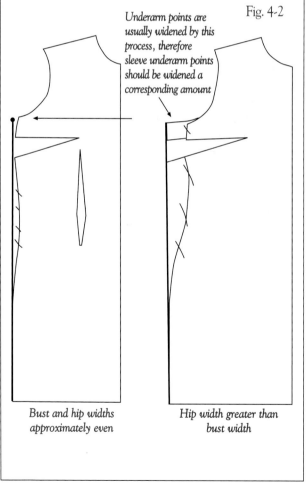

Squaring the side seam with the hem line

TO ADD OR NOT TO ADD SEAM ALLOWANCES TO YOUR PATTERNS

All patterns are drafted net, or without seam allowances. When you get ready to cut out the fashion garments, you may either add seam allowances to your pattern, or skip that step and mark both the sewing line and the cutting line on the fabric. The latter is the preferred method for two main reasons: it's faster and more accurate. Using the cut edge as a sewing guide on any but the firmest fabrics often provides a less precisely sewn seam—the more fluid the fabric, the more trouble you'll have. However, if you want to add the allowances to your patterns, it's best to add small (1/4 to 3/8 inch) ones to avoid distortion—assuming you're not planning to ever "let out" the seam. I never add seam allowances to my patterns. Instead, I use transfer paper and an adjustable double tracing wheel, which marks both the stitching and cutting lines anywhere from 1/4 to 1 inch apart. I usually add 1-inch seam allowances on the side seams of most garments to allow for future alterations. Never add more than a 5/8-inch seam allowance on jewel necklines, or on the bottom halves of basic armholes and crotch seams, because the fit will be compromised.

THE BASIC BLOCKS

These steps are not necessarily listed in each block's instructions, but they are applicable to each new draft:

1. Copy the base pattern you are starting from onto tracing paper.

2. Add extra ease to side seams, if desired, remembering to add the same amount equally to the front, back, and sleeve side seams when applicable. This ease may taper to zero at the waist, hip, or hem line, or may continue parallel to the side seam.

3. Mark new hem lines, if desired, at the same distance from the base pattern hem line on both the front and back.

4. Draw in the new style lines, dart locations, and cross marks where necessary.

5. Manipulate darts when applicable.

6. Copy the manipulated pattern onto a clean sheet of paper, marking the grain lines and all other pertinent information onto the copy.

7. True all seam lines by aligning them as they will be sewn.

8. Add seam allowances, if desired.

CONSTRUCTION GUIDELINES

For most garments, the following will serve as a step-by-step guide for construction, although the order of steps is somewhat variable. Think the construction through before beginning to sew and write down the steps for a quick reference if you like. Where applicable, follow these steps, pressing as needed:

1. Cut out and mark fabric. For those pattern pieces which require interfacing, apply the interfacing before marking that fabric pattern piece.

2. Sew darts where marked on all pattern pieces.

3. Combine any pieced sections so that you have a whole front and a whole back and apply any topstitching or embellishment to the pieced sections as desired.

4. Install pockets and/or bound buttonholes where applicable.

5. Sew the garment together at the shoulder seams and finish these seam allowances as desired.

6. Sew the front and back facing pieces together at the shoulder seams and finish the outside edge of the facing as desired.

7. Apply the facing to the garment.

8. To reduce bulk, trim (grade) the seam allowances of both the facing and the garment so that the seam allowance closest to the garment is slightly longer than the seam allowance that is closest to the facing.

9. Apply any desired topstitching to the garment opening.

10. For a set-in sleeve, sew the side seams of both the garment and sleeve. Finish these seam allowances as desired.

11. Install the sleeves and sleeve heads where used and trim the armhole seam allowance as follows: the upper half of the armhole is trimmed to 1/2 inch and the lower half is trimmed to 1/4 inch. Double-stitch the armhole seam to prevent its stretching.

12. For a separate kimono sleeve, sew the sleeve to the garment before sewing the side seams of the garment and sleeve.

13. Install the shoulder pads and tack any neckline facings.

14. Hem the garment and sleeves as desired.

THE INTERIM BLOCKS

STEP 1

A. Make a copy of your Bodymap Base Pattern from the waistline up. Use your compass to draw a circle around the bust point with a radius equal to the subject's bust radius (refer to the Pattern Drafting Personal Measurement Chart).

B. Draw straight lines radiating from the bust point to the following locations:

1. Shoulder point
2. Mid-shoulder (use the natural shoulder line)
3. Mid-neck
4. Center front
5. Armhole
6. Waistline (because the waist dart interferes, simply use the dart legs as the guideline as described below)

These straight lines form the centers of the contour guidelines listed below, which you will copy onto your pattern. At the point where the first three guidelines meet the bust radius circle, shade in a narrow wedge in the appropriate amounts, tapering to zero at both the bust point and the originating seam line for Guidelines 1 and 3, and ending at the bust radius for 2. Guideline 2 is only used for strapless designs.

Guideline 1: 5/8 inch   Guideline 2: 5/8 inch   Guideline 3: 5/8 inch
For Guideline 4, make a wedge that's 3/4 inch at the CF line, tapering to zero at the bust point.
For Guideline 5, make a wedge that's 1/4 inch at the armhole, tapering to zero at the bust point.
For Guideline 6, widen the waist dart 3/8 inch on each side of the intersection of the bust radius circle and each dart leg, tapering to zero at both the bust point and the originating seam line.
These are average amounts of the inward curve of the chest area, in relation to the protrusion of the bust.

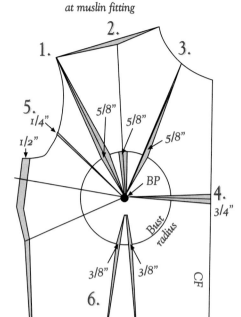

Shoulder contouring is done at muslin fitting

STEP 2

On the back, extend the waist dart to about mid-armhole level. Additionally, the side seams on contoured garments are brought in about 1/2 inch at the underarm points, tapering to zero at the waistline, and the mid-shoulders are contoured slightly as well, but these last adjustments can easily be made at a fitting. When drafting patterns in which a neckline has been lowered or the armhole is to be used for a sleeveless garment, the new style lines are drawn onto a copy of the contour block in pencil. Wherever they cross a contour guideline, the amount of wedge is measured and the pattern is adjusted accordingly. (See the tank top block top, page 94, as an example.) To facilitate the use of this pattern, make a copy of it and divide it into 8-1/2 x 11-inch sections (or 11 x 17-inch sections). Make photocopies and tape them together.

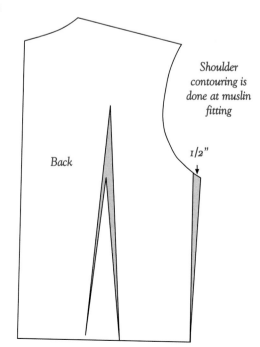

Back

Shoulder contouring is done at muslin fitting

This block is made for use with knits and other stretchy fabrics such as crinkled rayons or gauzes, for as the fabric "grows," so does the proper position of the pattern's crucial elements. These are just guidelines for adjustments and will vary depending on the firmness of the fabric.

STEP 1

Make a copy of your Bodymap Base Pattern. Move the bust point and its corresponding darts up (towards the shoulder seam) and in (towards CF) 1/4 inch.

STEP 2

Move the underarm points up 1/4 inch on both the front and back bodice and sleeve.

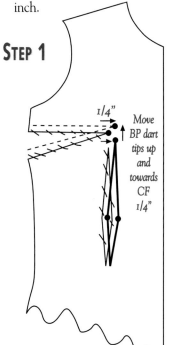

STEP 1

1/4"

Move BP dart tips up and towards CF 1/4"

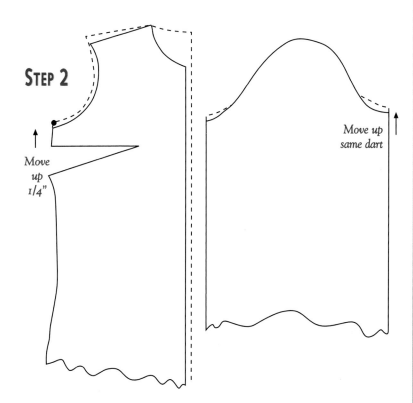

STEP 2

Move up 1/4"

Move up same dart

STEP 3

Reduce by 1/4" to 1/2"

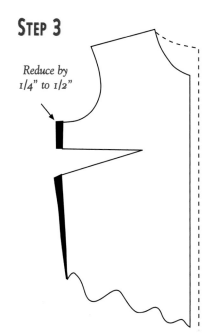

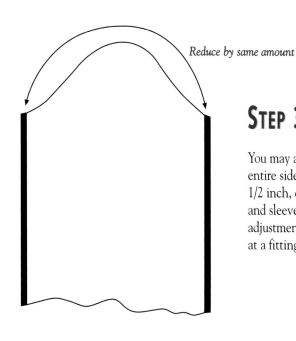

Reduce by same amount

STEP 3 (optional)

You may also move the entire side seam in 1/4 to 1/2 inch, on the front, back, and sleeves, but these adjustments could be made at a fitting.

EQUALIZED ARMHOLE BLOCK

This block is used as a starting point for kimono and raglan styles. Because the resulting over- and underarm seams in either pattern are extensions of the shoulder points and underarm points of the bodice, a longer back armhole would result in unattractively forward, and seemingly twisted, over- and underarm seam lines by the time they reach the wrist. To correct this, as well as to add ease for forward reach, you'll equalize the shoulder slope and then, when needed, pivot some or all of the bust dart into the armhole to make the front armhole as big as the back.

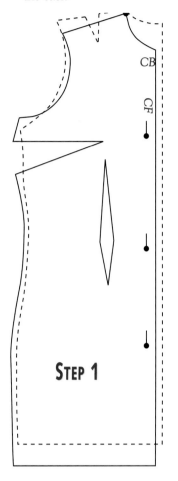

STEP 1

STEP 1

Make a copy of your Bodymap Base Pattern and pin your front and back patterns together with neck points touching and centerlines parallel. The back pattern may be longer than, shorter than, or equal to the front pattern when neck points are aligned.

STEP 2

Pivot the upper back dart into the armhole and cross it out. To do this, cut from the armhole to the dart tip and along the outer dart leg to the tip. Close the existing dart and open the new one in the armhole. Cross out this dart.

STEP 3

A. Equalize the shoulder slope by measuring the difference between the should tips. Subtract half of that distance from the higher side (usually the back) and add it to the lower side (usually the front) so they have the same slant.

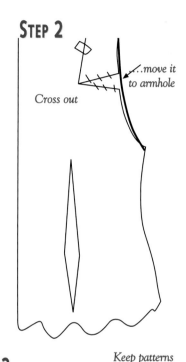

STEP 2

..move it to armhole

Cross out

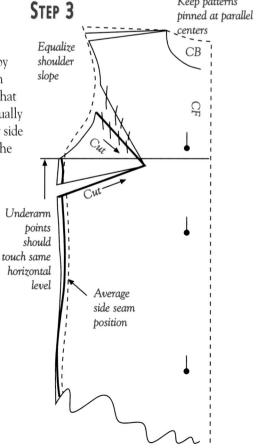

STEP 3

Keep patterns pinned at parallel centers

CB

CF

Equalize shoulder slope

Cut

Cut

Underarm points should touch same horizontal level

Average side seam position

B. Keep the patterns aligned at the neck points (and shoulder points after equalizing the slope) and check to see if the underarm points touch the same horizontal line. In most cases, they won't; the front underarm point will be higher. If so, cut from the mid-armhole and along the bottom dart leg of the existing dart to the bust point. Close the existing bust dart until the front underarm point touches the same cross grain line as the back underarm point (it may not be on the same vertical line because either the front or back pattern may be wider). This may close more than, or may not close, the original bust dart completely. If it doesn't close completely, patch the leftover bust dart and plan to use it in your garment. Measure the gap that appeared in the front armhole seam line, which is ease needed for front arm motion. If it's less than 1 inch, raise the shoulder points to incorporate this needed length.

C. If the underarm points don't align on the same vertical line, meaning that the front is wider than the back (or vice versa), average their position and draw a new side seam line underneath this averaged position, halfway between the front and back original side seam lines.

D. True the armholes and bust dart underlay.

STEP 4 (optional)

To create the equalized armhole block for princess line subjects, use a copy of the armhole princess line block (See page 79), cut apart the four panels, and attach the pattern pieces together at the armholes, pivoting the front and back side panels out diagonally. Equalize the shoulder slope as described, then lower the front underarm point by spreading the opening at the armhole until the front underarm point touches the same level as the back. Draw a revised princess seam line and average the side seam positions as described above.

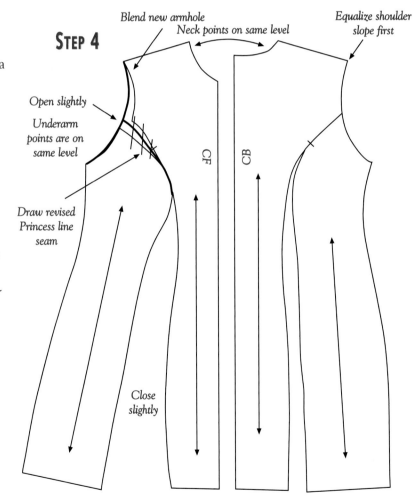

STEP 4

Blend new armhole

Neck points on same level

Equalize shoulder slope first

Open slightly

Underarm points are on same level

Draw revised Princess line seam

CF

CB

Close slightly

THE MANIPULATED BUST DART BLOCKS

The instructions for the French dart block can be used to move darts to any outside seam line surrounding the bust point; the only difference is the placement of the new dart positioning line.

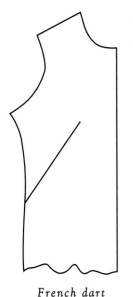

French dart block

STEP 1

A. Make a copy of your Bodymap Base Pattern. Draw a line from the lower side seam to the bust point. Ideally, this line will start at waist level, but its position can be varied. The lower along the side seam it begins, the wider the pattern piece will be.

B. Cut along this line and the lower dart leg line, to, but not through, the bust point and close the existing dart by joining the dart legs at the original dart position on the side seam, opening a dart lower down on the side seam.

STEP 1

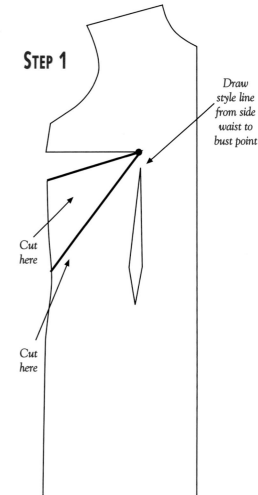

Draw style line from side waist to bust point

Cut here

Cut here

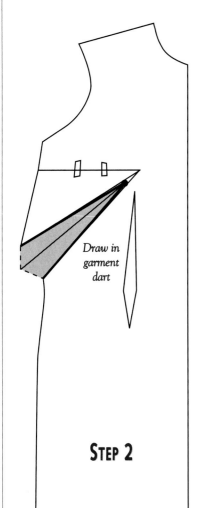

Draw in garment dart

STEP 2

STEP 2

A. Patch the opening with a scrap of tracing paper and draw in the garment dart tip at 3/4 inch from the bust point, along the dart's centerline.

B. Draw in the new dart by connecting the dart tip to the cut edges of the new dart opening at the side seam.

C. Fold out the dart, underlay going down, tape it closed, and true the side seam in order to achieve the correct dart underlay shaping.

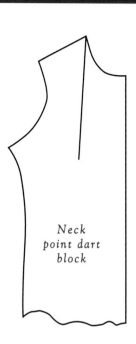

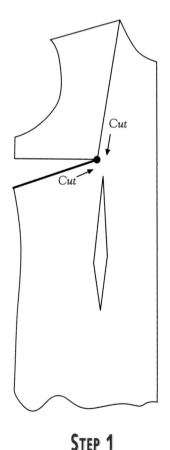

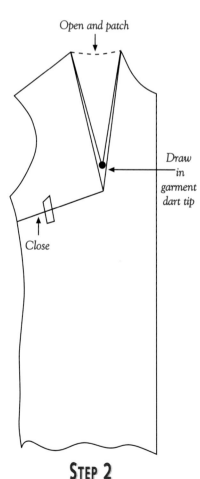

NECK POINT DART BLOCK

Stephanie wears the Florina Jacket, in a hand-painted and -quilted silk organza. The pattern is from the neck point dart block and has a shawl collar.

Neck point dart block

STEP 1

A. Make a copy of your Bodymap Base Pattern front. Draw a line from the neck point to the bust point.

B. Cut along this line and the lower dart leg line, to, but not through, the bust point and close the existing dart by joining the dart legs at the original dart position on the side seam, opening a dart at the neck point.

STEP 2

A. Patch the opening with a scrap of tracing paper and draw in the garment dart tip at 3/4 inch from the bust point, along the dart's centerline.

B. Draw in the new dart by connecting the dart tip to the cut edges of the new dart opening.

C. Fold out the dart, underlay going out towards the side, tape it closed, and true the shoulder seam in order to achieve the correct dart underlay shaping.

Cut

Cut

STEP 1

Open and patch

Draw in garment dart tip

Close

STEP 2

THE STYLE LINE BLOCKS

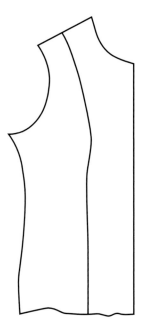

Shoulder princess
line block

Jennifer is in the Salonika Jacket, made of linen, over a rayon print tank top and pant. The jacket is a shoulder princess line with a cascade collar.

Darcy models the Adelaide dress, drafted from the shoulder princess line block with a square, contoured neckline and added flare in the skirt. It is made of a cotton jacquard.

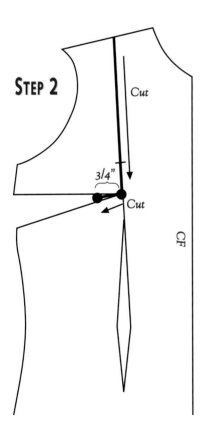

STEP 1

Line A

Draw in garment dart tip

1-1/2"
1-1/2"

Cross mark

CF

STEP 1

A. Make a copy of your Bodymap Base Pattern and draw on it the garment dart tip, which is 3/4 inch away from the bust point, along the dart's centerline.

B. Draw a straight line, "A," from the midpoint of the garment shoulder seam line to the waistline, passing through the bust point. Ideally, Line A will meet the waistline at the inner waist dart leg, but if not, you may reposition the waist dart by moving it slightly towards or away from CF, or you may start Line A to the left or right of the actual shoulder midpoint. Line A should be straight and pass through or within 1/4 inch of the bust point.

C. Cross mark this line at 1-1/2 inches above the bust point and cross mark each waist dart leg at 1-1/2 inches below the bust point.

STEP 2

Cut

3/4"

Cut

CF

STEP 2

Cut the pattern along Line A from the shoulder to the bust point and then cut from the bust point to the garment dart tip.

STEP 3

A. Close the garment dart to its tip, allowing a big gap to open at the shoulder and a small one to open between the bust point and the garment dart tip.

B. Patch the gaps with a scrap of tracing paper.

STEP 3

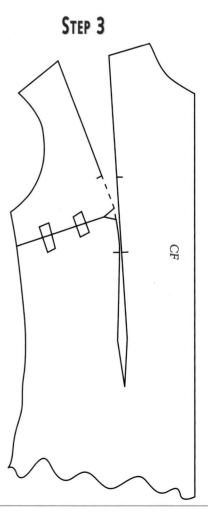

CF

STEP 4

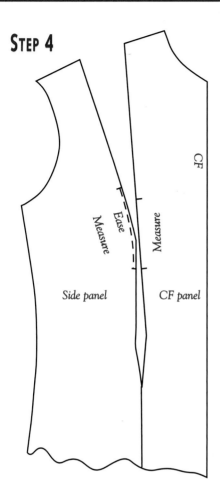

Side panel

CF panel

STEP 4

A. Blend the curve of the side panel in the bust area so it's a gentle curve there.

B. Mark "ease" between the cross marks and continue the princess style lines down to the hem line, going on both sides of the waist dart. The style line is perpendicular to the hem line.

C. Check the length of the seam lines between the cross marks on both the side panel and the CF panel. The side panel should be greater than or equal to the CF panel between the cross marks. If it's not, it has been blended too much and should be corrected. There's no need to separate this working block into individual panels; you'll do that on the fashion patterns used for actual garment making.

STEP 5

Reposition dart tip
if necessary

Blend

STEP 5

A. Transfer the position of the front princess line onto the shoulder seam line of the back pattern. (It might line up with the upper back dart legs, when applicable.)

B. With a French curve, connect this point to the waist dart tip (at underarm level) with a very shallow curve. Reposition the waist or upper back darts if necessary so this curve goes through the dart tips of each.

C. Cross mark at the levels of the dart tips and continue the style lines to the hem as you did the front pattern. Blend the side panel at the dart tip.

D. Separate the panels and align them from the upper cross mark to the shoulder seam line. You'll usually have to do this in tiny increments, by "walking" each seam line together as it will fit together when sewn. Tape them together and redraw the shoulder seam line, adding a patch of tracing paper if necessary.

Armhole princess block

Andrea's raw silk jacket, the Oakley, is based on the armhole princess line.

Linda is wearing the Victoria Jacket, from the armhole princess line block, in a rayon jacquard. Photo by Earl Gibson.

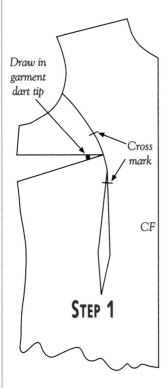

Draw in garment dart tip

Cross mark

CF

STEP 1

STEP 1

A. Make a copy of your Bodymap Base Pattern and draw on it the garment dart tip, which is 3/4 inches away from the bust point, along the dart's centerline.

B. With the help of a French curve, draw a curved style line from a point on the armhole (usually about mid-armhole) to the bust point.

C. Cross mark this line at 1-1/2 inches above the bust point and cross mark each waist dart leg at 1-1/2 inches below the bust point.

STEP 2

Cut the pattern along this curved style line to the bust point, then from the bust point to the garment dart tip, 3/4 inch away.

STEP 3

Close the garment dart to its tip, allowing a big gap to open at the armhole and a small one to open between the bust point and the garment dart tip.

STEP 4

A. Blend the curve of the side panel in the bust area so it's a gentle curve there.

B. Mark "ease" between the cross marks of the side panel and continue the princess style lines down to the hem line, going on both sides of the waist dart. Below the dart tip, the style line is perpendicular to the hem line.

C. Check the length of the seam lines between the cross marks on both the side panel and the CF panel. The side panel should be greater than or equal to the CF panel between the cross marks. If it's not, it has been blended too much and should be corrected. There's no need to separate this working block into individual panels; you'll do that on the fashion patterns used for actual garment making.

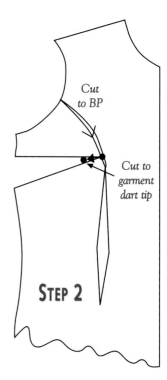

Cut to BP

Cut to garment dart tip

STEP 2

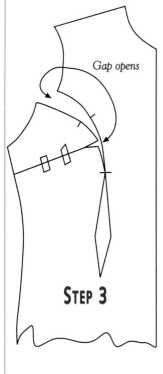

Gap opens

STEP 3

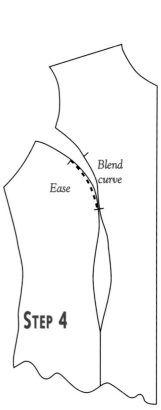

Ease

Blend curve

STEP 4

STEP 5

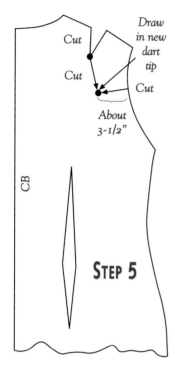

Draw in new dart tip

Cut

Cut

Cut

About 3-1/2"

CB

STEP 5

A. On the back pattern, draw in a new upper back dart tip at 3-1/2 inches from the armhole, at about an inch above mid-armhole level. (This level is variable.)

B. Cut along the inside upper back dart leg to its tip, then from its tip to the new dart tip. Cut from the armhole to, but not through, the new dart tip and close the original dart, opening a new dart in the armhole.

C. Patch this dart and measure the opening that occurred at the armhole.

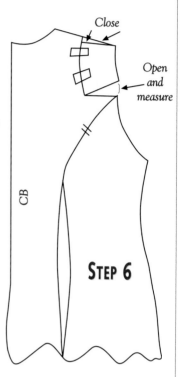

Close

Open and measure

CB

STEP 6

STEP 6

A. Draw a curved style line from the new dart's lower leg to the tip of the waist dart. You may want to reposition the waist dart (by moving it left or right, and/or lowering its tip) if the resulting style line is too curved.

B. Cross mark the style line at about halfway between the armhole and the waist dart tip.

C. Continue the style line down (perpendicularly) to the hem line, as you did the front.

STEP 7

Connect the upper armhole dart leg to the cross mark with a shallow curve. Widen this opening if it does not equal the same gap you measured in Step 6.

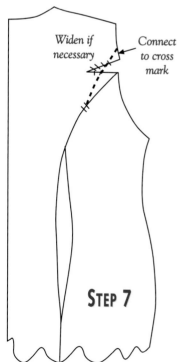

Widen if necessary

Connect to cross mark

STEP 7

STEP 8

A. True the armhole by first aligning the CB and side panels from the cross mark to the armhole along the princess style line. (You should cut the pattern to separate the panels first.) You'll usually have to do this in tiny increments, by "walking" each seam line together as it will fit together when sewn.

B. Tape the pattern pieces together at the armhole and connect the shoulder point to the armhole of the side back panel.

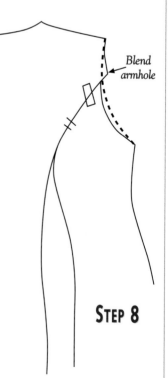

Blend armhole

STEP 8

PANEL STYLE LINE BLOCK

STEP 1

A. Make a copy of your Bodymap Base Pattern. At midpoint between the side seam and the bust point, draw a vertical line from the armhole to the hem line. (The position of this line is somewhat variable; it can be an inch or so closer to the bust point if you wish.)

B. From the upper dart leg, gently curve this line into the armhole and cross mark the style line above and below the bust.

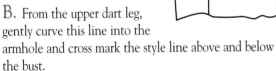

Panel style line block

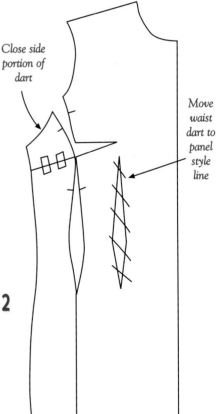

Kathy is all-business in the Wexford jacket, from the panel style line block. It has a notched collar and is made of a silk mattka.

STEP 2

A. Cut along the panel style line to the lower dart leg and close the dart from the side seam to the style line.

B. Reposition the waist dart horizontally so it is bisected by the panel style line and blend the seam lines, continuing the style line perpendicularly to the hem line.

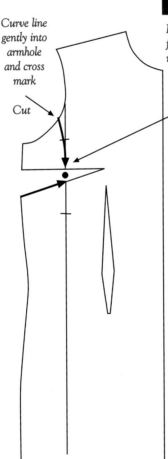

Curve line gently into armhole and cross mark

Cut

STEP 1

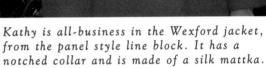

At mid-dart, draw a vertical line from armhole to hem line

Close side portion of dart

Move waist dart to panel style line

STEP 2

STEP 3

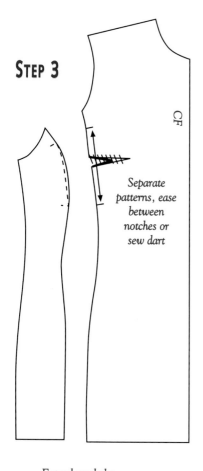

Separate patterns, ease between notches or sew dart

STEP 3

A. Blend the style line in the dart curve area of the side panel and separate the pattern pieces.

B. Cross out the remaining dart portion on the CF panel, marking "ease" between its cross marks. To retain the proper bust shaping, the CF panel should be eased between the cross marks so its length is reduced to equal the side panel.

STEP 4

A. On the back, draw in the panel style line at about the same distance from the underarm point as on the front and curve it into the armhole as well.

B. Move the waist dart to the new style line as you did on the front and blend all lines.

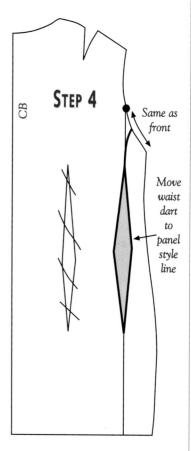

Step 4

Same as front

Move waist dart to panel style line

STEP 5

Extend armholes so they touch

Side back *Side front*

Join side panels at full hip

STEP 5 (optional)

A. To eliminate the side seam, adjoin the side panels together at the hip, cross out the side waist shaping, and extend the underarm points if they don't meet.

B. Measure any increase to the armhole caused by extending the underarm points and add the same amount of extension to the sleeve underarm points.

C. Fine-tune the waist dart depth and length at a fitting and remeasure the armholes before drafting your sleeve.

Note: For a less shaped, more traditional menswear-styled jacket, you may start with a base pattern in which you've pivoted a maximum of 5/8 inch of the bust dart angle into the armhole. To do this, draw a line from the bust point to the mid-armhole. Cross mark this line at 3 inches from the bust point. Cut along this line and along the lower bust dart leg, to, but not through, the bust point and close the bust dart until the gap at the 3-inch mark is 5/8 inch wide. Patch the opening and blend the armhole.

Note: If the fashion fabric shows ripples when eased, sew the remaining dart as a triangular dart, after marking the garment dart tip, or draft the pattern with the style line closer to the bust point. (Larger-than-average bust dart angles may need one of these adjustments on many fabrics.)

YOKE STYLE LINE BLOCK

STEP 1

A. Make a copy of your Bodymap Base Pattern. Draw in the front yoke style line about 1-1/2 inches below and parallel to the shoulder seam line.

B. Cross mark and remove the yoke section.

Yoke style line block

STEP 2

A. Draw a line from the bust point to the midpoint of the yoke line, then draw two parallel lines 1 inch away and on either side of this line. Stop these lines 1 inch away from the bust point, then angle them over to the bust point.

B. Cut along each of the three parallel lines and the lower dart leg, to, but not through, the bust point.

Nettie is in the Kildare Tunic, with a back opening, in a poly/cotton knit with twin needle stitching detail. It is a variation of the yoke style line block, with the curved yoke going through the bust point.

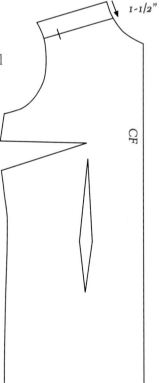

STEP 1

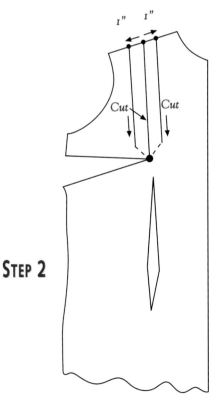

STEP 2

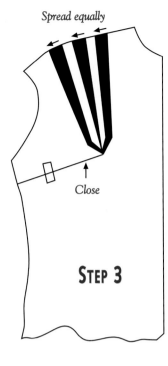

Spread equally

Close

STEP 3

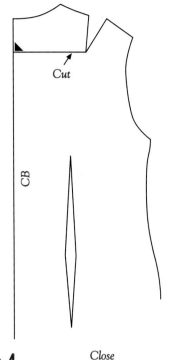

Cut

CB

STEP 3

A. Close the side bust dart, spreading each opening equally at the yoke seam line.

B. Mark the pleat directions of the new dart and patch and true the dart underlay, or you may gather this seam between the openings.

STEP 4

A. On the back, square a line from the CB line to the level of the upper back dart tip. Cut along this line and close the upper back dart, then continue the straight line to the armhole and cut away the rest of the back yoke.

B. Blend the lower back section.

STEP 4

Close

Continue cutting to armhole

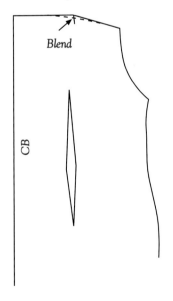

Blend

CB

STEP 5

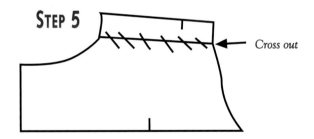

Cross out

STEP 5

Tape the shoulder lines of the front and back yoke sections together and cross out the original shoulder line.

THE COMBINATION BLOCKS

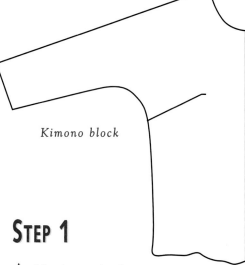

Kimono block

STEP 1

A. Use the equalized armhole block. Align the front and back patterns with neck and shoulder points touching and centerlines parallel.

Linda is wearing the Toulouse Tunic, made of hand-dyed silk jacquard and silk chiffon. It is based on the kimono block with separate sleeves and has a scarf front.

B. Lay a double layer of tracing paper on top of the patterns so you can draft the kimono patterns onto them.

The length is equal to the straight sleeve measurement, minus 1/2"

4" to 5" or more

Connect to underarm point and blend into curve

CF

C. Cross mark the shoulder point. You may add extra ease to the shoulder by raising the shoulder point 1/2 inch or more before continuing. Measure the centerline of the straight sleeve pattern from the top of the cap to the hem line to get the total sleeve measurement. Subtract 1/2 inch from the total sleeve length and extend the shoulder seam line straight out this amount.

D. At the endpoint of this line, square a line that extends down 4 to 5 inches (or more, if you want a wider wrist hem line).

E. Connect the bottom of the sleeve hem line to the underarm point of the bodice and blend the underarm curve smoothly. If the side bust dart extends into the sleeve portion, transfer it to a lower side seam position, like a French dart (See page 74). Close the bust dart and true the side seams.

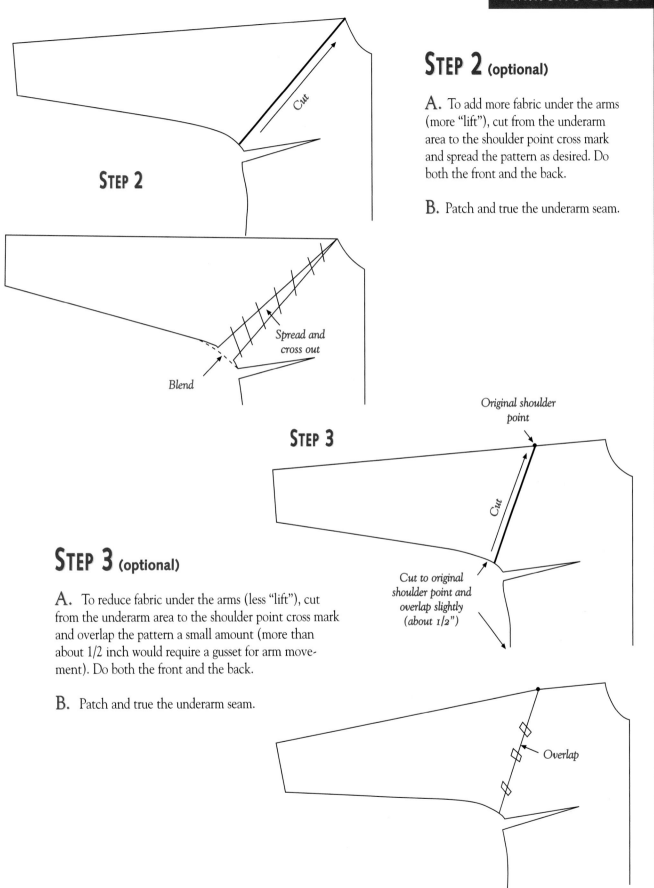

STEP 2

STEP 2 (optional)

A. To add more fabric under the arms (more "lift"), cut from the underarm area to the shoulder point cross mark and spread the pattern as desired. Do both the front and the back.

B. Patch and true the underarm seam.

Spread and cross out

Blend

STEP 3

Original shoulder point

Cut

Cut to original shoulder point and overlap slightly (about 1/2")

STEP 3 (optional)

A. To reduce fabric under the arms (less "lift"), cut from the underarm area to the shoulder point cross mark and overlap the pattern a small amount (more than about 1/2 inch would require a gusset for arm movement). Do both the front and the back.

B. Patch and true the underarm seam.

Overlap

STEP 4 (optional)

A. For a separate sleeve, align the front and back patterns along the shoulder (over-arm) seam line.

B. Square a line to the over-arm seam in the desired location, usually just past the main part of the underarm curve.

C. Mark the shoulder point cross mark onto the sleeve and separate the pattern pieces.

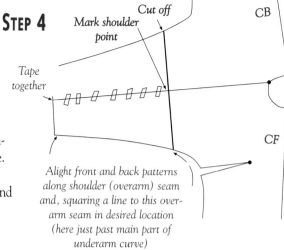

STEP 4

Cut off

Mark shoulder point

CB

Tape together

CF

Alight front and back patterns along shoulder (overarm) seam and, squaring a line to this over-arm seam in desired location (here just past main part of underarm curve)

STEP 5 (optional)

For a separate mock-raglan sleeve, combine the front and back patterns as in Step 4, but draw in the separate sleeve arcing from the underarm area to the neckline in raglan fashion.

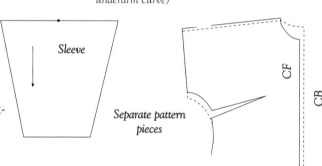

Sleeve

Separate pattern pieces

CF

CB

STEP 6 (optional)

To convert a princess line pattern to kimono, align the equalized armhole princess line patterns with armholes joined and draw a shoulder princess style line from the bust point to the mid-shoulder in front and from the tip of the waist dart to the mid-shoulder in back. Cross out the armhole style lines and draft the kimono pattern as described.

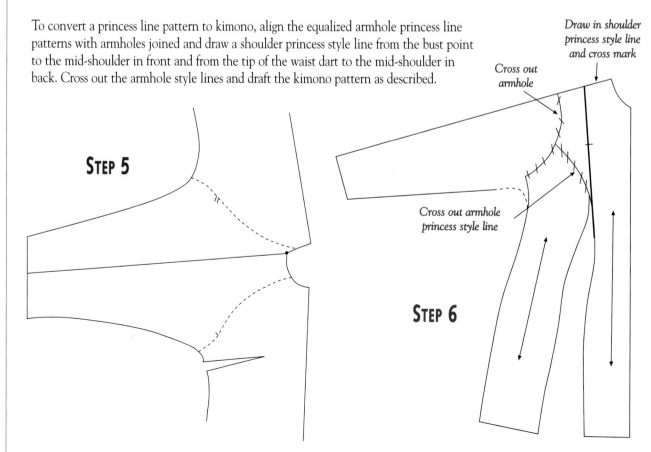

STEP 5

Draw in shoulder princess style line and cross mark

Cross out armhole

Cross out armhole princess style line

STEP 6

*Note: This draft contains a one-piece sleeve with a shoulder dart forming the shoulder slope, as opposed to a two-piece sleeve with an over-arm seam. If you want the over-arm seam, or if you plan to draft the princess-raglan bodice (see optional Steps 5 and 6), you **must** use the equalized armhole pattern, which loses some of the bust shaping, as your starting point. This draft retains all of the bust and upper back darts.*

Raglan-sleeved block

Linda's top is the Valencia Tunic, from the raglan sleeve block, with a variation of the cascade collar used as a cowl inset. It is made of a rayon jacquard.

Kathy's Greenleaf tunic comes from the raglan sleeve block and has a fold-over turtleneck collar. The neckline has been widened and lowered so that it pulls over the head. Like its matching skirt, it is constructed of a poly/cotton knit.

STEP 1

A. Make a copy of your Bodymap Base Pattern and your straight or shaped sleeve block. Mark a new neck point on the front and back necklines that's about 1 to 1-1/2 inches down from the neck points.

B. Mark a match point on the armholes that's 3 to 4 inches up from the underarm point, marking the same distance on both the front and the back armholes.

C. Connect the new neck points to the armhole match points with straight lines and, at the midpoint of the lines, square up 1/2 inch and mark point C.

D. Draw in the raglan style line by connecting the new neck points to the armhole match points, passing through C. Cross mark the raglan style lines.

E. On the straight sleeve block, mark the armhole points at the same distance from the underarm points as on the bodice.

STEP 2

A. Cut away the raglan sections from the front and back bodices

B. Lengthen the upper back dart to the raglan style line, then close the back dart.

C. Blend the raglan style line.

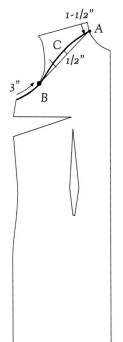

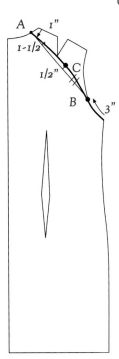

STEP 1

Connect A to B at midpoint of AB; square up 1/2", label C, and connect A, C, B with gentle curve

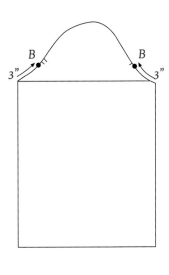

Close dart

Blend off any point that may occur here

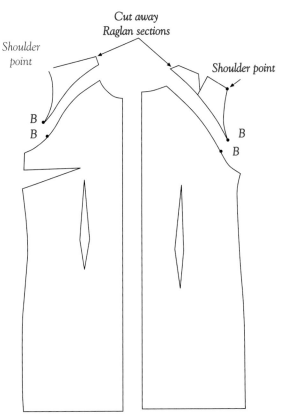

Cut away Raglan sections

Shoulder point

Shoulder point

STEP 2

STEP 3

A. Attach the raglan sections to the sleeve pattern with the armhole marks touching and the straight shoulder lines converging on the sleeve cap seam line (they won't meet).

B. Connect the original neck points on the raglan sections to the sleeve, gently arcing over the shoulder points to converge at a point 5/8 to 1 inch below the cap seam line.

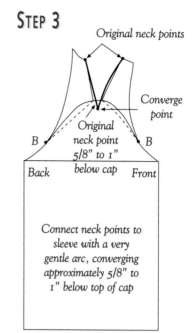

STEP 3

Original neck points

Converge point

Original neck point 5/8" to 1" below cap

B — *Back*   B — *Front*

Connect neck points to sleeve with a very gentle arc, converging approximately 5/8" to 1" below top of cap

STEP 4

A. Patch the opening between the shoulder seam dart (the dart formed by the raglan sections) and fold the paper so that the neck points are touching. Continue the fold to the converging point.

B. Blend the shoulder seam dart with the help of a French curve, moving the converging point down slightly if it makes a smoother line.

STEP 5 (optional)

If you used the equalized armhole block, you may separate the sleeve along its centerline and taper the sleeve hem line equally on each side, if desired. You may add an elbow dart as well. (See page 63)

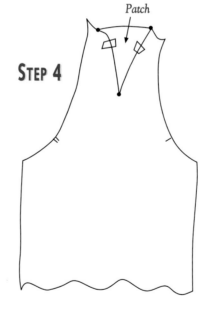

Patch

STEP 4

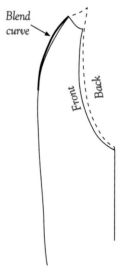

Blend curve

Front   *Back*

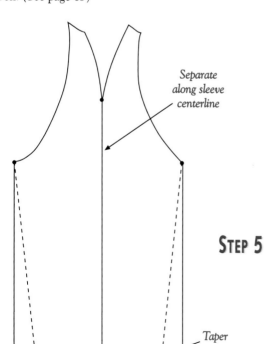

Separate along sleeve centerline

STEP 5

Taper

STEP 6 (optional)

To create the princess raglan pattern, use the equalized armhole block you developed from a princess line pattern. (See page 73)

A. With the patterns taped together at the armholes, draft the raglan style lines and sleeves as described above and redraw the front and back princess style lines if needed so they originate at the same distance from the underarm point as on the raglan sleeve (point B).

B. Separate the sleeve into front and back sections along the sleeve centerline.

C. On the front pattern, tape the sleeve to the bodice along the raglan line so that the neckline is whole again and the armhole match points (B) on both the bodice and sleeve are touching. Cross out the raglan style lines from the armhole match points to the neckline. Cut away the side panel, leaving the CF panel and the sleeve combined.

D. Repeat this process on the back pattern.

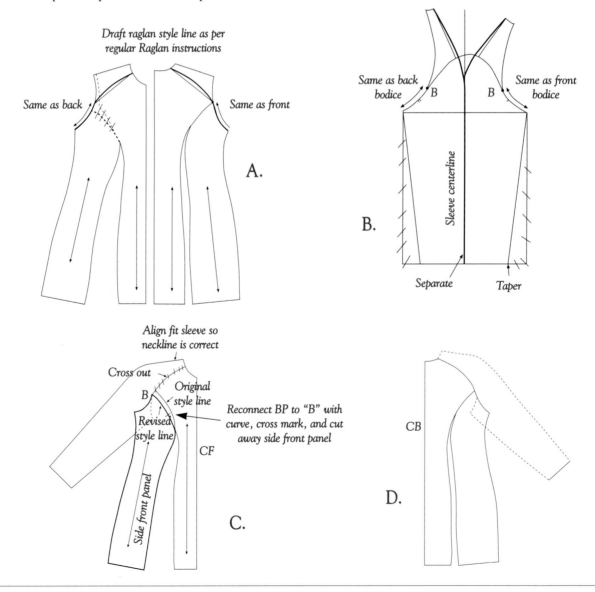

This block is called a "mock" dropped shoulder, because, while it creates a better dropped shoulder look than traditional dropped shoulder drafts (no bubbles at the sleeve cap/shoulder junction), it is really a kimono block with a fisheye (double-ended) dart in the underarm area.

Mock-dropped shoulder block

STEP 1

A. Tape the front and back kimono blocks together along the over-arm seam and cover them with tracing paper.

B. Trace all markings onto the tracing paper and remove the kimono blocks.

C. Mark a new shoulder point about 2 inches out from the shoulder point cross mark.

D. Connect this point to the underarm curve with a straight line, "A." Draw in the fisheye dart from the midpoint of Line A to the underarm curve, its width about 1/2 to 3/4 inch at the dart center.

STEP 2

A. Blend the bodice armhole into a gentle concave curve and the sleeve into a smooth sleeve shape along the dart lines.

B. Cross mark the shoulder point onto the sleeve and separate it from the bodice.

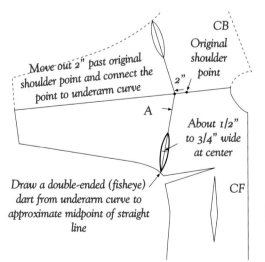

Lorie relaxes in a cotton gauze bathing suit cover-up. The pattern is derived from the mock-dropped shoulder block and has a cascade collar.

Move out 2" past original shoulder point and connect the point to underarm curve

CB
Original shoulder point

2"

A

About 1/2" to 3/4" wide at center

Draw a double-ended (fisheye) dart from underarm curve to approximate midpoint of straight line

CF

STEP 1

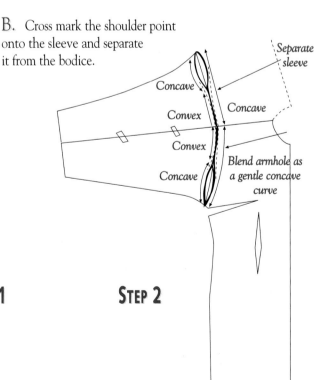

Separate sleeve

Concave

Convex

Concave

Convex

Concave

Blend armhole as a gentle concave curve

STEP 2

THE SLEEVELESS BLOCKS

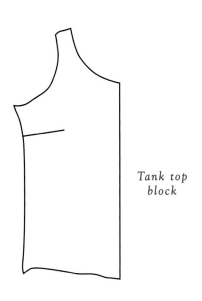

Tank top
block

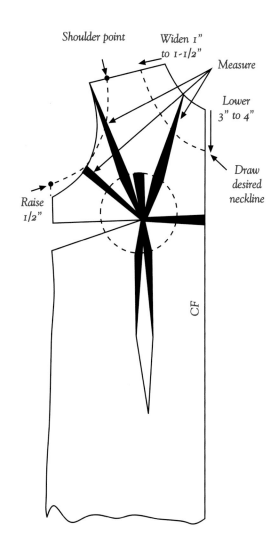

Shoulder point

Widen 1"
to 1-1/2"

Measure

Lower
3" to 4"

Draw
desired
neckline

Raise
1/2"

CF

Kathy is comfortable in the Marseille top, which is the tank top block lengthened to mid-calf. It is constructed of a crinkled rayon. Vests can be derived from this block by deepening the armholes and adding a center front opening. Photo by Earl Gibson.

STEP 1

A. Make a copy of your Contour Guideline Pattern front and your Bodymap Base Pattern back. On the front, pencil in the desired neckline shape. To do this, widen the neckline by 1 to 1-1/2 inches and lower it as desired, usually about 3 to 4 inches.

B. Mark the shoulder point at the desired distance from the new neck point (on the natural shoulder line, without the shoulder pad adjustment), usually about 2 to 3 inches away.

C. Raise the underarm point 1/2 inch and draw in the new armhole, passing through the front draping point.

D. Measure the amount of contouring where the new neckline and armhole cross the contour guidelines.

STEP 2

A. Cut to the bust point along each affected guideline and along the lower dart leg and overlap the guidelines the measured amount, widening the bust dart.

B. Draw in the garment dart.

C. Contour the side seam by 1/2 inch at the underarm point, tapering to zero at the waist.

D. You may contour the mid-shoulder seam now or after a muslin fitting.

STEP 3

A. On the back, transfer the upper back dart to the neckline. (See page 72)

B. Tape the front to the back at the shoulder seam and draw in the back neckline, connecting it smoothly with the new front neckline and lowering it so it falls below the tip of the neckline dart.

C. Raise the underarm point 1/2 inch and draw in the new armhole, passing through the back draping point.

STEP 4 (optional)

A. You may contour the back armhole if you wish by cutting from mid-armhole to mid-neckline and overlapping the armhole seam line by 1/4 inch.

B. True the neckline.

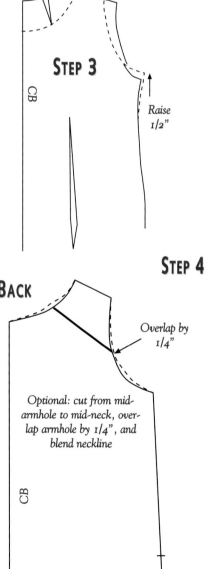

Overlap

STEP 2

Widen same as front   *Front*   *Widen*

CF

Widen same as front

CB

STEP 3

Raise 1/2"

STEP 4

CB

Overlap by 1/4"

Optional: cut from mid-armhole to mid-neck, overlap armhole by 1/4", and blend neckline

CB

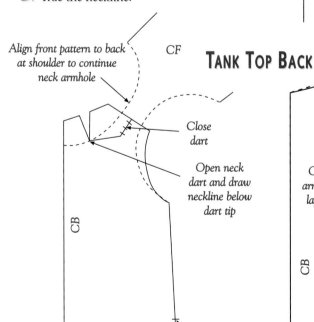

Align front pattern to back at shoulder to continue neck armhole

CF

TANK TOP BACK

Close dart

Open neck dart and draw neckline below dart tip

CB

Mark "slit" location

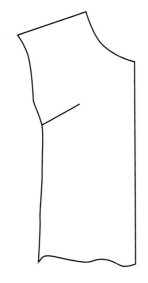

*Cap-
sleeved
block*

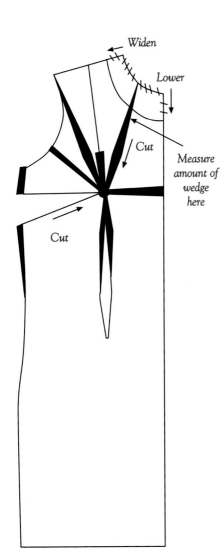

Widen

Lower

Cut

Measure
amount of
wedge
here

Cut

*Lorie wears the San Miguel Top, from the cap-
sleeved block, in a printed poly/cotton rib knit,
over a matching skirt.*

STEP 1

A. Make a copy of your Contour Guideline Pattern front and your Bodymap Base Pattern back. On the front, pencil in the desired neckline shape. To do this, widen the neckline by 1 to 1-1/2 inches and lower it as desired, usually about 3 to 4 inches.

B. Measure the amount of contouring where the new neckline crosses the contour guidelines.

C. Cut to the bust point along the mid-neck guideline and along the lower dart leg.

STEP 2

A. Overlap the guideline the measured amount, widening the bust dart. Note: Because the cap sleeve armhole is outside of the draping points, there is no requirement for armhole contouring.

B. Draw a line from the bust point to mid-armhole.

C. Cross mark this line at 3 inches from the bust point.

STEP 3

A. Cut along this line and along the lower bust dart leg, to, but not through, the bust point and close the bust dart until the gap at the 3-inch mark is 5/8 inch wide.

B. Patch the opening.

C. Cross out the armhole and its dart.

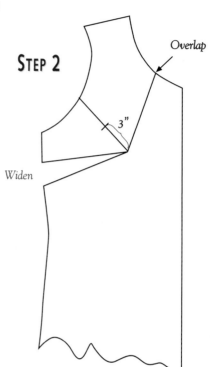

STEP 2

Overlap

3"

Widen

STEP 4

A. Draw in the garment dart.

B. Raise the shoulder point 1/4 inch.

C. Extend the underarm point vertically until it's higher than the neck point level.

D. Connect the new neck point to the underarm point extension line, passing through the raised shoulder point and ending at "A," 1 inch wider than the underarm point extension line.

E. Draw in the new armhole by connecting "A" to the underarm point with a shallow curve.

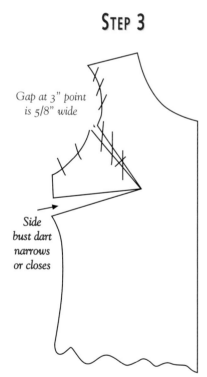

STEP 3

Gap at 3" point is 5/8" wide

Side bust dart narrows or closes

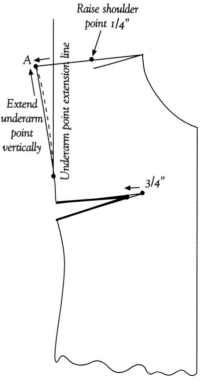

STEP 4

Raise shoulder point 1/4"

A

Underarm point extension line

Extend underarm point vertically

3/4"

STEP 5

A. On the back, pivot the upper back dart to the armhole (See page 72), leaving it open.
B. Widen the back neckline the same as you did the front neckline and lower it as desired, usually 1 to 2 inches.
C. Cross out the armhole and its dart.
D. Raise the shoulder point 1/4 inch.

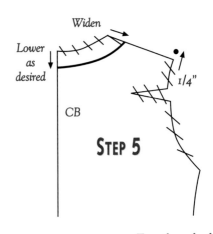

Widen

Lower as desired

CB

1/4"

STEP 5

STEP 6

A. Align the front pattern over the back pattern with new neck points and raised shoulder points together. The CF and CB may or may not be parallel, depending on the original shoulder slant and armhole size.
B. Trace the front shoulder line arc onto the back pattern, making the shoulder lines the same length.

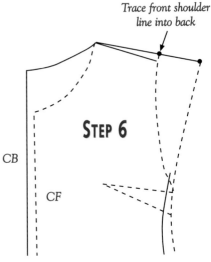

Trace front shoulder line into back

CB

CF

STEP 6

STEP 7

Align the patterns at the ends of the shoulder seams and true the armhole, blending the front smoothly into the back underarm point. This may shorten the shoulder seam.

STEP 8 (optional)

A. You may widen the underarm points after truing the armhole seam.
B. You may taper the shoulder sleeve from the raised shoulder point to the armhole into a shallow arc.

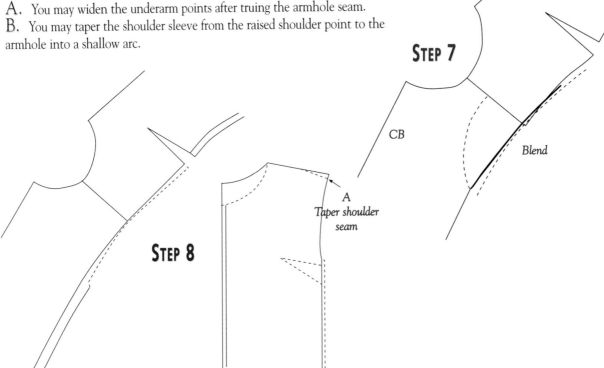

CF

STEP 7

CB

Blend

A
Taper shoulder seam

STEP 8

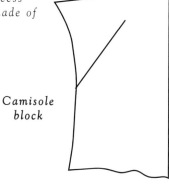

Andrea is in the Kea Camisole, made of a beautiful rayon scarf, from the camisole block. It is worn under an armhole princess line jacket made of silk mattka.

Camisole
block

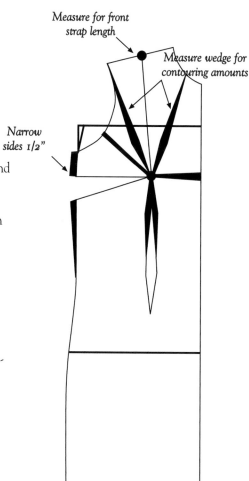

Measure for front strap length

Measure wedge for contouring amounts

Narrow sides 1/2"

STEP 1

A. Make a copy of your Contour Guideline Pattern, front and back, and narrow the side seams by 1/2 inch from underarm point to waistline.

B. Mark a horizontal neckline at the desired level, usually about 1 inch above the border of the bust radius.

C. From the new neckline, draw a straight line to the shoulder midpoint.

D. Measure this for the approximate front strap length.

E. Measure the amount of contouring on both the mid-neck and shoulder point guidelines to be applied.

STEP 2

Transfer the bust dart to French dart position. (See page 74)

STEP 3

A. Cut along each guideline and along the lower dart leg to the bust point. Overlap the guidelines the measured amounts and patch the widened bust dart.

B. Square the neckline to the CF line, making sure its length hasn't changed. Draw in the garment dart.

STEP 4

A. With the bust dart folded out, align the side seam of the front pattern with the side seam of the back pattern and mark the new underarm point on the back.

B. At this level, draw in the back neckline, squared to the CB line.

C. Measure from the midpoint of the back neckline to the shoulder midpoint to determine the back strap length.

D. Adjust the strap length and neckline levels at a muslin fitting.

STEP 2

Contour guidelines

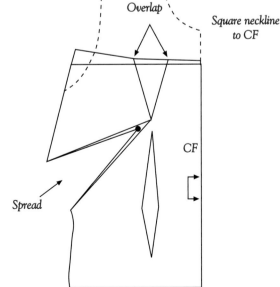

STEP 3

Overlap

Square neckline to CF

CF

Spread

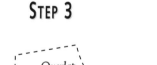

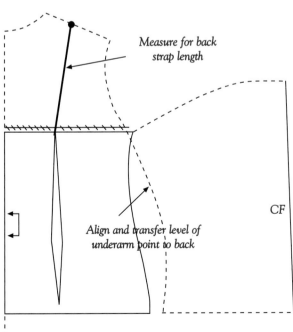

STEP 4

Measure for back strap length

Align and transfer level of underarm point to back

CF

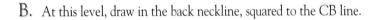

COLLAR BLOCKS

Just as you measure the garment armholes to draft a sleeve, you also must measure the garment neckline to draft a collar. Unless there has been fullness added, like for a gathered collar, the collar's neckline equals the garment's neckline in a 1:1 ratio where they are sewn together. The outer edge of the collar is much more variable in length and can be adjusted by adding or subtracting wedges along it, as you'll see in some of the drafts described below. There are two main parts to a collar: the "stand," the part of the collar that goes up the neck from the neckline, and the "fall," the part of the collar that falls from the neck over the stand. The fold line that divides the two parts is called the "roll line."

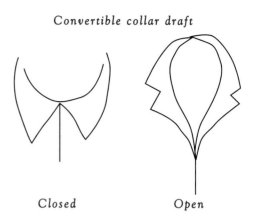

Convertible collar draft

Closed   *Open*

This collar, the basic "shirt" collar, can be worn open or closed, hence the name "convertible."

STEP 1

A. Measure the neckline from the CB to the CF, noting the distance from the CB to the shoulder point. (Do not include the overlap width.)

B. Draw a rectangle that's the width of the collar (example: 3 inches) by the neckline measurement.

C. Mark the shoulder point and label the collar's CF and CB. Raise the CF point 1/2 inch and connect this new neckline to the shoulder point, then trim away the original portion. Extend the top of the collar out past CF 1 inch (or more) and connect this to the new CF neck point. Blend the shoulder point.

STEP 2

Shape the collar front edge as desired.

STEP 1

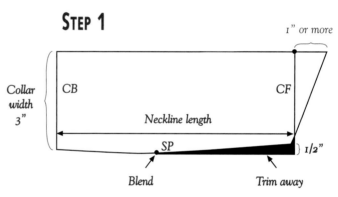

Collar width 3"

CB   CF

Neckline length

1" or more

SP

Blend   Trim away

1/2"

STEP 2

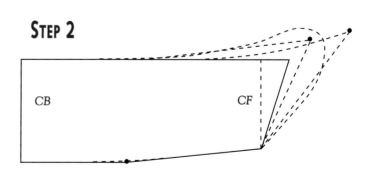

CB   CF

MANDARIN COLLAR DRAFT

Also called a "band" or "stand" collar, this collar has no fall and can meet at the CF, at the edge of the overlap, or it can stop short of the CF. This draft is for a CF meeting.

Mandarin collar draft

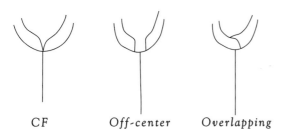

CF   Off-center   Overlapping

Kathy is wearing the Santa Cruz jacket, in a hand-painted, -embroidered, and -beaded silk organza. It is based on the kimono block with separate sleeves and has a mandarin collar. Photo by Earl Gibson.

STEP 1

A. Measure the front and back necklines and draw a rectangle with a length equal to the total neckline and the desired width (example: 1-1/4 inches).

B. Mark the shoulder point and draw in the CF collar shape. (The shape is usually squared, angled, or rounded.)

STEP 2

Cut from the upper edge of the collar, to, but not through, the shoulder point and overlap this cut by 1/4 inch. Blend the collar seam lines.

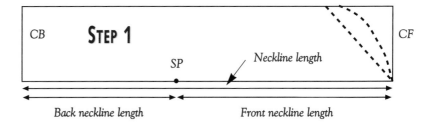

CB   **STEP 1**   SP   Neckline length   CF

Back neckline length   Front neckline length

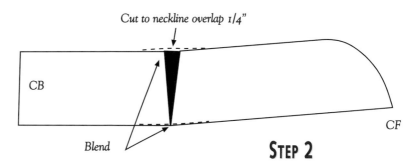

Cut to neckline overlap 1/4"

CB   CF

Blend   **STEP 2**

Andrea enjoys this kimono-sleeved Autumn jacket, made of a linen jacquard. Her top has a bias fold-over turtleneck collar.

The first draft is for a jewel (basic) neckline with a CB opening. The second draft is for widened and lowered necklines which can be pulled over the head (most commonly used with knits).

Fold-over turtleneck collar draft

DRAFT 1 - STEP 1

A. Measure the neckline from the CB to the CF, noting the distance from the CB to the shoulder point.

B. Draw a rectangle that's equal to quadruple the width of the collar (example: 4 x 2 = 8 inches) by the neckline measurement.

C. Label the CF, CB, and shoulder point.

D. Cut CF on the fold.

STEP 2

A. For woven fabrics, make a whole pattern and mark the CF on the bias grain line. Knits can have the CF on the bias or straight grain.

B. Add a back overlap, if desired. (Or, the CB could meet and be held closed with hooks and eyes or loops and buttons.)

STEP 1

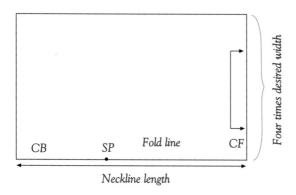

STEP 2

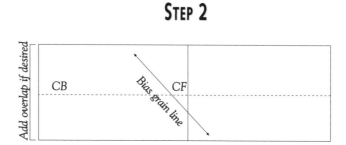

DRAFT 2 - STEP 1

Widen the garment neckline by about 1 inch, lower the CF 1-1/4 inches, and lower the CB 1/2 inch. If this is to be used as a pull-over, check to make sure that the neckline will fit over your head. To do this, make a circle of your tape measure, the length of which is equal to the garment neckline, and try to pull it over your head. Widen and lower the neckline more if needed.

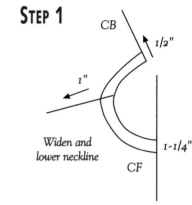

STEP 1

CB

1/2"

1"

Widen and lower neckline

CF

1-1/4"

STEP 2

A. Draft the basic collar, following the steps listed in Draft 1, Step 1 above, doubling instead of quadrupling the desired width. This example uses a collar width of 6-1/2 inches for a slouchy effect.

B. On the CF line, measure down the amount the front neckline was lowered (ex. 1-1/4 inch) and extend the CF to this point.

C. On the CB line, measure down the amount the neckline was lowered (ex. 1/2 inch) and extend the CB line to this point.

D. Connect these points to the shoulder point with straight lines, then blend with a French curve as pictured.

E. Mirror image these extensions on the other edge of the collar, so that when the collar is folded in half, the cut edges will be shaped the same.

F. Mark the CF line on the fold.

G. Measure the revised (curved) neckline of the collar, which may have increased slightly.

STEP 3

Adjust the collar length by cutting the collar apart vertically at the shoulder point. Overlap the collar until its neckline equals that of the garment. Reposition the shoulder point if necessary.

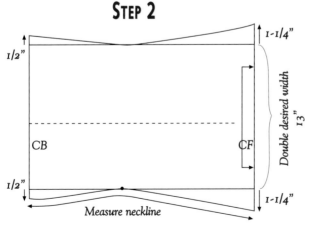

STEP 2

1/2"

1-1/4"

Double desired width
13"

CB

CF

1/2"

Measure neckline

1-1/4"

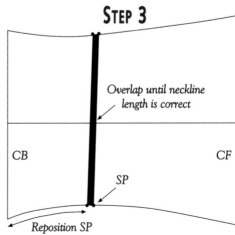

STEP 3

Overlap until neckline length is correct

CB

CF

SP

Reposition SP

The shawl collar has a seam at the CB and forms both the collar and the lapel of the garment.

STEP 1

A. To the bodice, add the button overlap and mark the breakpoint at the level of the top button. (The breakpoint is where the lapel starts its turn back over the front of the garment.)

B. Square a line from the shoulder seam, its length equal to the back neckline, and square a line from this line, its length equal to the width of the collar (example: 3 inches).

Andrea is in the reversible Telluride Jacket, based on the kimono block with separate sleeves. It has a shawl collar and is made of a Pendleton Wool blanket fabric.

C. To mark the collar stand point at CB, divide the collar width by 2 and subtract 1/4 inch. (Here, 3 divided by 2 equals 1-1/2, minus 1/4 inch = 1-1/4.)

D. Move out on the collar width line this distance from the CB neck point and dot. Connect this dot to the breakpoint and label this diagonal line the roll line.

E. Draw in the desired collar shape, connecting the end of the CB seam line to the breakpoint, here in a gentle curve.

STEP 2

A. Cut from the collar edge to the neck point and from the collar edge to the back line and spread these cuts 1/4 to 3/8 inch each.

B. Patch and true the collar and neckline edges.

C. For a collar that sits a bit lower on the front part of the neck, draw in a double-ended (fisheye) dart from the neck point to a point about 1/2 inch from the roll line, its width about 1/2 inch (optional).

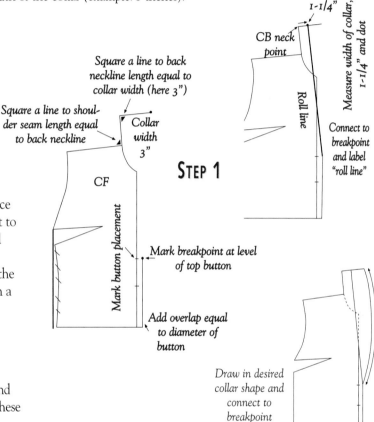

Shawl collar draft

Square a line to back neckline length equal to collar width (here 3")

Square a line to shoulder seam length equal to back neckline

Collar width 3"

CF

Mark button placement

STEP 1

Mark breakpoint at level of top button

Add overlap equal to diameter of button

1-1/4"

CB neck point

Roll line

Measure width of collar, 1-1/4" and dot

Connect to breakpoint and label "roll line"

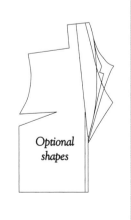

Draw in desired collar shape and connect to breakpoint

Optional shapes

For a more comfortable fit at neckline, draw in a fisheye dart from neck point to 1/2" from roll line

STEP 2

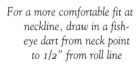

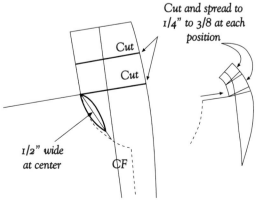

Cut

Cut

Cut and spread to 1/4" to 3/8 at each position

1/2" wide at center

CF

Notched collar draft

STEP 1

A. Draft a shawl collar as described in the shawl collar instructions above, leaving the original front neckline (but not the fisheye dart) marked.

B. Place the notch point at either the original CF neck point or slightly outside of it, towards the collar edge.

STEP 2

Fold the pattern on the roll line from the breakpoint to the neck and draw in the desired notch shape.

STEP 3

A. Trim away the notched area and cut the collar from its outside edge (about 1-1/2 inches above the notch) to, but not through, the original neckline/roll line intersection.

B. Cut the collar from the neck point to, but not through, this same intersection.

STEP 4

Spread the collar edge until the neck point of the garment is overlapped by 1/4 to 3/8 inch by the collar.

STEP 5

A. Patch, separate, and true the collar.

B. Cut the under collar as two separate pieces with the CB on the bias and the upper collar with the CB on the fold of the straight grain.

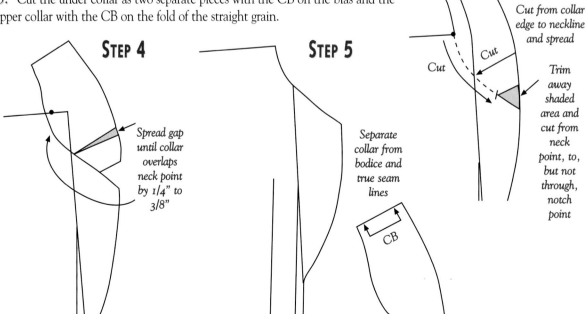

STEP 1

Place notch point at original CF neck point or slightly past

CF neck point

STEP 2

Fold over on roll line and draw in desired notch and collar shape

STEP 3

Cut from collar edge to neckline and spread

Cut

Cut

Trim away shaded area and cut from neck point, to, but not through, notch point

STEP 4

Spread gap until collar overlaps neck point by 1/4" to 3/8"

STEP 5

Separate collar from bodice and true seam lines

CB

CASCADE COLLAR

Cindi is wearing the Bella Jacket, drafted from the kimono and cascade collar blocks, made of hand-dyed silk organza. She wears the Rafaela Tunic, also derived from the kimono block, with the cascade collar used as a cowl inset under it. It is made of a matching silk jacquard. Both pieces are bound in a double layer of metallic gold grosgrain ribbon.

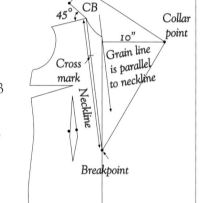

Cascade collar draft

Cowl inset (Cascade collar)

This collar is a shawl collar variation.

STEP 1

STEP 1

A. Draw the back neckline at a 45° angle to the front shoulder line and square the CB line to this line, its length equal to the desired collar width (example: 3 inches).

B. From the CF line, at a level anywhere between the CF neck point and midway between the neck point and the bust line, square out a 10-inch line. Dot the position of the collar point.

C. Connect this collar point to the CB edge of the collar.

D. Draw in the breakpoint on the CF line about 3 inches below the waistline and connect to the collar point with a straight line.

E. Connect the breakpoint to the neck point of the garment and cross mark this line. This line forms the collar edge and the neckline of the garment.

F. Mark the grain line of the collar parallel to the neckline. This will stop the neckline, which is bias, from stretching.

STEP 2 (optional)

STEP 3

STEP 2

Alternatively, you could draft the collar edge squared from the CB line as well and use the lower edge of the collar on the straight of grain (See Step 3A below). You can also shape the outer edge of the collar in numerous ways.

STEP 3 (optional)

This collar can be used as an inset cowl. To do this:

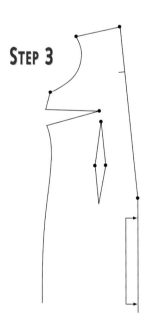

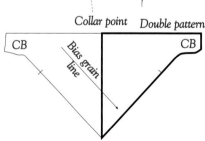

A. Draft it the same as the cascade collar, except square it from the collar point to the CB line.

B. Make a copy of it doubled.

C. Use the resulting pattern centerline as the CF and mark the grain line on the bias.

D. Use the same neckline as on the cascade collar draft and cut the lower CF of the bodice on the fold, or with a seam.

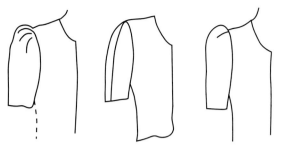

Sleeve with raised cap block

If you want to use a shorter shoulder seam length than specified by your garment shoulder seam measurement, add cap height to the sleeve in this manner:

STEP 1

At about 1-1/2 inches on either side of the cap point (shoulder match point of the sleeve cap), cut down 2 inches and then cut to, but not through, the underarm seam on each side.

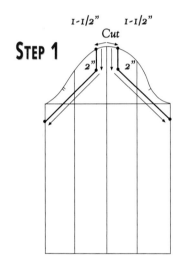

STEP 2

A. Raise and spread the cap sections apart until the cap height has been extended to the amount the shoulder seam was shortened (or more for a higher gathered cap).
B. Move the section containing the cap point up the same amount.
C. Mark "gather" between the crease lines.
D. Straighten the side seams. Notice that this also adds width to the bicep line.

OR - STEP 3 (optional)

Mark pleats going out.

OR - STEP 4 (optional)

Create an over-arm seam. Measure the amount of space opened up and move it to either side of the shoulder match point.

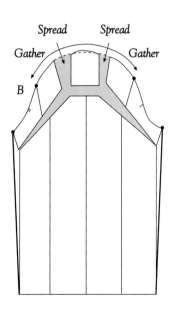

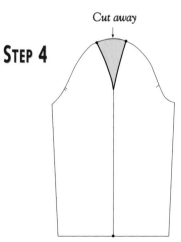

STEP 1

A. Make a copy of the straight sleeve block, including the crease lines that divide the pattern into fourths (add ease at the sides if the bodice was changed).

B. Fold the sleeve pattern in half, with underarm seams meeting in the center.

C. Tape the underarm seam together along its full length.

D. Draw a line "A," midpoint between the front fold line and the underarm seam.

Two-part shaped sleeve block

STEP 2

A. From back to front, cut the elbow line through all layers, to, but not through, the front fold line.

B. Spread the back fold line apart until the gap under the elbow line equals the difference between the front and back arm measurements listed on the Pattern Drafting Personal Measurement Chart.

C. On each side, patch the gap with a scrap of paper.

D. Measure in on the hem line 1 inch from the back fold line, and mark "B."

E. Connect B with the lower elbow line on the back fold line and trim the excess paper away.

F. Label the back arm seam line "C." Redraw the elbow line at the original level, parallel to the bicep line.

G. Square the hem line from C at B, touching the front fold line slightly above the original hem line.

H. Trim away the excess paper from below this revised hem line.

I. Cross mark Lines A and C at 2 inches above and 2 inches below the elbow line.

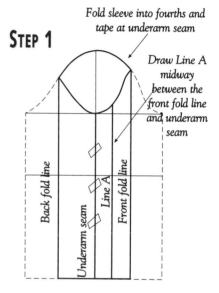

Fold sleeve into fourths and tape at underarm seam

STEP 1

Draw Line A midway between the front fold line and underarm seam

STEP 3

A. Separate the upper sleeve from the lower sleeve by cutting along Lines A and C.

B. Unfold the upper sleeve. You'll notice that there is a bubble that occurs at the elbow line/front fold line and that the pattern will not lie flat.

C. Cut into this bubble to Line A and overlap it so it does lie flat.

D. Mark "stretch" between the cross marks. (When sewing the sleeve, you'll need to stretch this portion in order for the cross marks to align with those on the under sleeve. On fabrics with little stretch, this may not be possible, and you should draft the sleeve with the lengths of Line A equal on the upper and under sleeve.)

STEP 2

Redraw elbow line and cross mark C and A

Spread apart and patch

Trim away excess

Square hem line to Line C

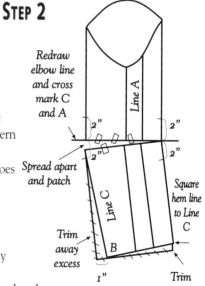

Bicep line

Front fold line

Line A

Overlap

Cut to fold line and overlap Line A at elbow

STEP 3

STEP 4

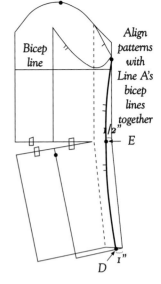

STEP 4

A. Align the two pattern pieces with "A" lines together and bicep lines matching.
B. Measure in on the hem line 1 inch from Line A and mark "D."
C. Measure in on the elbow line 1/2 inch from Line A and mark "E."
D. Connect D, E, and the top of the seam line at the sleeve cap with a gentle curve, making sure not to narrow the bicep line.

STEP 5

A. Cut the patterns apart on this curved line.
B. With bottom cross marks aligned on A, true the hem line of the upper sleeve by blending it into the under sleeve hem line at A.

STEP 6

A. To add extra ease to the bicep line, patch a piece of tracing paper to the back arm seams of both pattern pieces.
B. Extend the bicep lines out 3/8 inch each and connect the sleeve cap line to the elbow line through this point with a gentle curve.
C. Add a vent, if desired, usually 3 inches by 1-1/2 inches.

STEP 7 (optional)

A. To hide the back arm seam, before adding the extra ease to the bicep lines, tape the under sleeve and the upper sleeve together along the back arm seam line from the sleeve cap line to the elbow line.
B. Draw the revised back arm seam line. To do this, on the under sleeve, mark a point on the cap seam line that's about 1 inch from the back arm seam line. Connect this point to the elbow line at the back seam line and cross out the original back arm seam line, using the new line as the correct back arm seam line.
C. Add additional ease to the sleeve as described above.

STEP 5

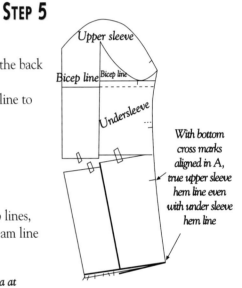

With bottom cross marks aligned in A, true upper sleeve hem line even with under sleeve hem line

STEP 6

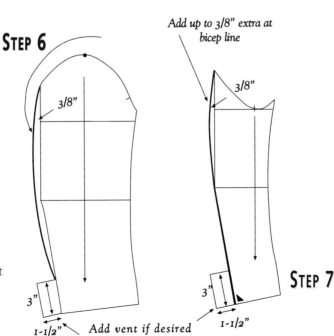

3/8"

Add up to 3/8" extra at bicep line

3/8"

3"

1-1/2" Add vent if desired

3"

1-1/2"

STEP 7

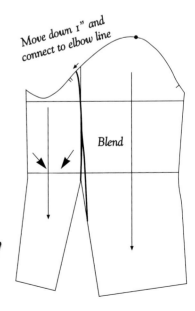

Move down 1" and connect to elbow line

Blend

The linen Coventry Shirt that Valarie wears was drafted using the yoke style line block, the shirt sleeve with cuff, and the convertible collar.

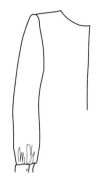

Shirt sleeve with cuff block

STEP 1

A. Copy the straight sleeve block and taper the wrist, if desired.

B. Curve the hem line to allow for the curve of the arm. To do this, lower the hem line at the center of the sleeve and both of the underarm seam points by 1/2 inch and lower the back crease line by 1 inch.

C. Leave the front fold line hem level as is and connect these points with the help of a French curve.

STEP 1

Taper   *Taper*

1/2"   1"   *1/2"*

STEP 2

A. Subtract 1/2 inch from the cuff width (example: 2 inches) and shorten the sleeve this amount.

B. Mark a 3-inch long wrist opening on the back fold line.

C. Mark gathering lines from the slit to each side seam.

D. Taper wrist, if desired.

STEP 3 (optional)

A. If you desire to pleat the sleeve into the cuff rather than gather it, mark the position of the first pleat at the sleeve center and the second pleat halfway between here and the sleeve opening. Mark a third, if desired, on the other side of the sleeve opening.

B. The pleat take-up depends on the sleeve and cuff width. To figure it, subtract the cuff width including any over- and under-lap) from the sleeve hem line width and divide it by the number of pleats.

STEP 2

For 2" wide cuff cut off 1-1/2" from sleeve bottom

Mark gathering line

3"   *1-1/2"*

STEP 4

A. To draft the cuff, draw a rectangle that's the cuff width (example: 2 inches) by the desired length (usually wrist plus 1/2 to 1 inch).

B. Add the button overlap and under-lap (equal to button diameter) on each side.

C. Cross mark the position where the underarm seam will join the cuff at 1/4 the length of the net cuff (from the back of the cuff).

D. Mark the buttonhole and button positions equidistant from the top and bottom of the cuff (example: 5/8 inch). Place the bottom of the cuff on the fold.

Sleeve center

STEP 3

3"   2"   1"

Pleat positions

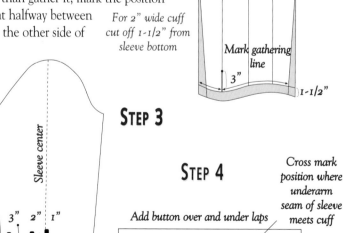

STEP 4

Cross mark position where underarm seam of sleeve meets cuff

Add button over and under laps

Front   Back

Cut 2" on fold

Place on fold

Wrist plus 1/2 to 1"

BUTTON OVERLAP AND PLACEMENT

To add the overlap, also called "button stand" or "extension," decide on the size button you want to use. Use the following as guidelines for the width of the overlap: (1) For buttons up to and including 3/4 inch in diameter, the overlap equals the diameter of the button. (2) For buttons over 3/4 inch, the overlap equals 1/2 the button diameter plus 1/4 to 1/2 inch, as desired. To add the overlap:

STEP 1

Determine the width of the overlap and, at this distance outside of the line of closure (usually the CF or CB), draw a parallel line.

STEP 2

Mark the position of the first buttonhole by measuring down from the neckline seam line a distance of half the diameter of the buttonhole, plus 1/4 to 3/8 inch. The buttonhole placement line starts 1/8 inch out from the closure line, on the overlap extension (or slightly farther out if the holes of the button or shank are considerably wider) and extends into the garment. The length of the buttonhole is usually the diameter of the button plus 1/8 to 1/4 inch, depending on the button's thickness.

STEP 3

A. Determine the number of buttons wanted. Try to position a button at both the bust line and waistline levels.

B. Mark the position of the first and last buttonholes.

C. Measure the distance between the first and last buttonholes. Divide this figure by the number of spaces to determine the distance between each button. (The number of spaces is equal to the number of buttons minus 1, for singular button placement.)

D. Mark the positions of the other buttonholes. Mark the positions of the buttons, at the same level of the buttonhole, on the closure line. On women's garments, the buttonholes go on the right side of the front, the left side of the back. On men's garments, these positions are reversed.

Always do a test buttonhole.

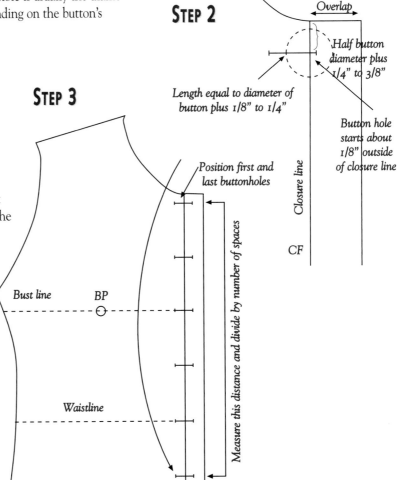

STEP 1

CF (closure line)

Width of overlap

STEP 2

Overlap

Half button diameter plus 1/4" to 3/8"

Length equal to diameter of button plus 1/8" to 1/4"

Button hole starts about 1/8" outside of closure line

Closure line

CF

STEP 3

Position first and last buttonholes

Bust line   BP

Waistline

Measure this distance and divide by number of spaces

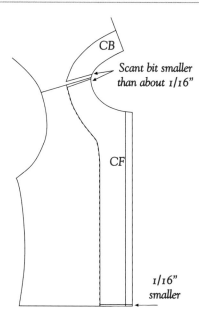

CB

Scant bit smaller
than about 1/16"

CF

1/16"
smaller

FACINGS

Facings are used to finish curved or shaped garment edges such as necklines, hem lines, and armholes on sleeveless garments, whenever a fold-over hem is inappropriate. A facing's outer edge is essentially a mirror image of the edge it's facing. When "hidden," meaning that the facing is turned to the underside of the garment, not to be seen, it is cut a scant bit smaller in length and pressed under far enough so that it will not make its presence known. Before sewing the bottom of the facing to the garment hem line, always place the garment on a hanger or dress form, allowing the facing to fall naturally. Pin in place and sew accordingly.

ADDING FULLNESS

Volumes could be written about this pattern-making principle, because the applications are truly endless. Added fullness is applied in one of three ways:

1. Equal fullness, where the fullness added to one side of the pattern piece equals that added to the other. For example, as a CB pleat below the yoke of a basic shirt.

2. One-sided fullness, where the fullness is added to one side of a pattern piece but tapers to zero added on the other side, or before it reaches the other side. For example, as a flared panel of a princess line dress.

3. Unequal fullness, where fullness is added to both sides of a pattern piece, but in uneven amounts. For example, on the gathered skirt of a traditional wedding dress.

In determining which of the three methods you should employ, ask yourself, "Where do I want the fullness?" Because, in the same way that a bust dart pivoted into the armhole and left open will show up as a diagonal fold there, where you put fullness is where it will remain.

Equal fullness   *Added fullness*

1.

CB   CB

*Fullness is
equal from
top to bottom*

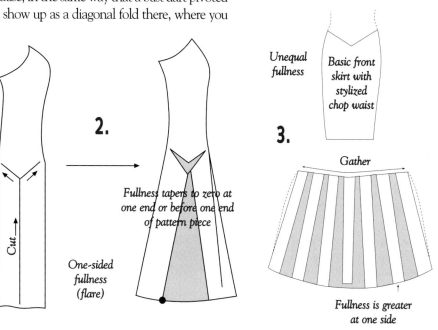

2.

Cut

*One-sided
fullness
(flare)*

*Fullness tapers to zero at
one end or before one end
of pattern piece*

*Unequal
fullness*

*Basic front
skirt with
stylized
chop waist*

3.

Gather

*Fullness is greater
at one side*

APPENDIX 1
DART ANGLE COMPARISON

TO ANALYZE THE GRAIN-CONTROLLING DART ANGLES:

Compare the example of the right side of the body to the left by adding the dart angles together, per side:

Right bust	2-1/2"	Left bust	1-3/4"
Right shoulder slope	2-3/4"	Left shoulder slope	3"
Right upper back	3/4"	Left upper back	3/4"
	6"		5-1/2"

In this case, it seems that the right side has a larger bust dart angle, a smaller shoulder slope dart angle, and an equal upper back dart angle. Does this mean that the right breast is bigger than the left and that the right shoulder is higher than the left? It could, but more than likely some of the bust dart was shifted into the shoulder slope dart on the left side, or vice versa on the right side. The overall difference, because it exceeds 1/4 inch, probably indicates that some part of the right body does require more shape than the left side. If it is a shape imbalance, it could either be in the shoulder area or in the bust area, and you need to determine which. In this case, it may be that the right shoulder is slightly higher than the left shoulder. You can double-check this by evaluating some of the other markings on the Bodymap. Start with the shoulder pin markings nearest the neck edge of the gingham—they will be farther apart from front to back and the gingham-to-weighted rope measurement will have been different. On the lower side, the gingham would have been farther away, and the original shoulder slope darts, if drawn as pinned, would have converged farther inside the neck opening.

Other telltale signs of a lowered shoulder are a lower bust point and/or a lower underarm level on the suspected lower side. If any of these three factors exist, then the shoulders are probably asymmetrical. If none of these factors exist, however, it's possible that one breast is actually bigger than the other. This condition is very common, but with the exception of very close fitting garments, like a strapless cocktail dress, rarely does the difference require different sized bust darts. If the difference in the bust dart angles exceeds 1/2 inch, with all other angles being equal, you should evaluate the subject visually to determine whether or not the breasts are obviously so different in size that a variance in bust dart size is necessary. Ideally, the subject will choose to simply pad up the smaller side, an extremely time-saving solution with regard to

pattern-making, because the alternative is to draft and cut each side of the front singly for each pattern.

At any rate, once you've determined that there is an imbalance, you must make some choices with regard to future pattern-making. You can choose to make separate right and left patterns (or simply mark the differences on one pattern), you can cut the two sides symmetrically and pad up the lower side where applicable, or you can ignore the imbalance. In the case of shoulders, a lower one is usually accompanied by a lower neck point, because the shoulder is usually lowered by a compression in the rib area, rather than a malformation in the actual shoulder. Therefore, a shoulder pad, which tapers to nothing at the neck point, will not be able to "pad up" the neck edge of the shoulder seam, and may result in gaping at the neck on that side. In some cases, however, the imbalance is a result of muscular development and could be helped with either a shoulder pad or by lowering both the shoulder point and underarm point an equal amount, so that the armhole remains the same size. A symmetrically cut test garment would help you to determine which is the case. Ignoring the imbalance may have unforeseen consequences in addition to the slight diagonal folds that will occur on the side of the lower shoulder, because quite often the center of the garment will swing off kilter as well.

In the interest of streamlining the sewing process, a symmetrically cut pattern would be the choice to make if the differences are small. Pull up the bra strap, pad that bra cup if you need to, increase the shoulder pad height, and disregard a slightly looser neckline on the low side. The following section is intended for those with major asymmetries, who desire a perfect pattern for each side of the body. Circle the angles you'll use (choosing the smaller ones) in the Dart Angle Comparison Chart (page 42).

If you decide that the shoulders are asymmetrical and the

subject wants the pattern marked accordingly, make the bust darts and the shoulder blade darts equal from right to left by transferring any difference into the shoulder slope dart. Use the lower of the two numbers as the corrected dart angle. In this case, the bust dart would be 1-3/4 inches, and move the difference of 3/4 inch into the shoulder slope dart total on the right side.

Right bust	1-3/4"	Left bust	1-3/4"
Right shoulder slope	3-1/2"	Left shoulder slope	3"
Right upper back	3/4"	Left upper back	3/4"
	6"		5-1/2"

Then deduct 1/4 inch that you're disregarding from the larger shoulder slope angle and use this as your corrected dart angle for that side.

Right bust	1-3/4"	Left bust	1-3/4"
Right shoulder slope	3-1/4"	Left shoulder slope	3"
Right upper back	3/4"	Left upper back	3/4"
	5-3/4"		5-1/2"

If you decide that the breasts are asymmetrical and the subject wants different sized bust darts on either side, make the other darts equal from side to side, using the lower of the angles, and move any difference to the bust dart on the appropriate side.

Right bust	2-1/2"	Left bust	2"
Right shoulder slope	2-3/4"	Left shoulder slope	2-3/4"
Right upper back	3/4"	Left upper back	3/4"
	6"		5-1/2"

Then deduct 1/4 inch that you're disregarding from the larger bust angle and use this as your corrected dart angle for that side. Note: The level of the bust points may also be different in some cases.

Right bust	2-1/4"	Left bust	2"
Right shoulder slope	2-3/4"	Left shoulder slope	2-3/4"
Right upper back	3/4"	Left upper back	3/4"
	5-3/4"		5-1/2"

If you decide that the shoulder blades are asymmetrical enough to merit different sized darts (which is pretty rare except in the case of certain back deformities such as scoliosis, which is often accompanied by uneven shoulders), make the bust darts equal from side to side and move any difference (less the 1/4 inch you're disregarding) into the upper back dart on the appropriate side.

In any case, record the corrected dart angles in the appropriate spaces on the dart angle comparison chart. In this example, I'll make the bust and upper back darts equal each other on the left and right sides, choosing the smaller bust dart angle, and I'll move the difference of 3/4 inch into the shoulder slope dart, then I'll subtract the 1/4 inch. So my dart angles look like this:

Right bust	1-3/4"	Left bust	1-3/4"
Right shoulder slope	3-1/4"	Left shoulder slope	3"
Right upper back	3/4"	Left upper back	3/4"
	5-3/4"		5-1/2"

See page 56 for the asymmetry adjustment illustration.

APPENDIX 2
MAKING ASYMMETRY ADJUSTMENTS

If you need to make an adjustment for asymmetric shoulders, open out the front of the pattern and draw a line from the shoulder point of the higher shoulder to the side seam of the opposite side, about halfway between the underarm point and waist level. (Draw this line above the bust point unless the levels of the bust points were different enough to merit a separate bust point position, in which case you should draw the line below the bust point.) Because the subject's shoulder slope angles listed in Appendix 1 were measured at 3 inches from the neck point, you're going to lower that same point on the natural (no shoulder pad) shoulder line—3 inches from the neck point—by one-half of the correction amount. (The other half will be done on the back.) To do this, cut along the diagonal line from the underarm point to, but not through, the end of the shoulder point. Shift the top layer down until the marked 3 inch point on the shoulder seam line moves down the correct amount.

For example, if the difference in dart angles is 1/4 inch, the front correction amount would be 1/8 inch, and you'd move the 3-inch point down this amount. Tape the pattern together securely, add a small piece of paper to the side seam, and blend it from waist to underarm. Perform the same process on the back pattern piece, making sure you're lowering the same side as you did in the front. Redraw the CF and CB lines by connecting them from hem to the neck.

APPENDIX 3
BORROWING COLLARS, NECKLINES, AND CLOSURES FROM COMMERCIAL PATTERNS

Sewers usually select patterns for the details, and there's an easy way to incorporate those same details into sewn garments without having to test the fit over and over again. The Bodymapping process has resulted in perfectly-fitted patterns with the bust dart in various locations, which you can use as you like, according to your own design sense and garment requirements. You may choose any Bodymap Block and add any fashion pattern detail to it as you wish. For instance, you may decide that you'd like a particular collar on a raglan-sleeved, princess line dress, instead of the panel line jacket it was intended for, or that the neckline on a dress would look fabulous on a tunic. To achieve as close a match as possible, use the Bodymap block that most resembles the commercial pattern—use your side darted pattern when the fashion pattern is side darted, for example. (Those of you with top-to-bottom imbalances which require a princess line will use the princess line as your base pattern.) Just remember, it's smart to sketch any drastic changes before starting, to make sure all the elements will work together as you intend.

Incorporating the fashion pattern's details onto your Bodymap takes only a few steps. Necklines and collars, by far the most desired details, require that you first determine how the neckline has been changed from the sloper's basic jewel neck. Has the neckline been widened and/or lowered? If so, how much? Collars drafted for use with even a slightly widened or lowered neckline often perform a bit differently than those drafted for a jewel neck, so you need to follow the same steps the pattern designer did in order to achieve the exact same effect. But how can you tell if it's been widened? You must compare the neck widths of the fashion pattern and the pattern company's sloper it was derived from—the same sized sloper as the pattern you're using. Then you must compare the neck widths of your *personal* sloper and the pattern company's sloper, because this is a very common area of discrepancy between real bodies and the standard bodies upon which the patterns have been based. As mentioned in Chapter 1, many personal neck widths are much narrower than those upon which commercial patterns are based. Therefore, the neck width of the fashion pattern must be adjusted in order to trace off the neckline properly. It is only after the neckline has been corrected to fit your size that the collar can be adjusted and copied. For these reasons, I've included neck width measurement charts for every size available from every major pattern company which offers a fitting shell (see page 119).

The collar from a Vogue blouse pattern was borrowed and added to the basic side darted design, with eliminated waist darts. This blouse is made of a silk charmeuse print.

Hopefully you'll see why borrowing details is the fastest and easiest way to use commercial fashion patterns for your garment sewing. If you're using a pattern from a company not listed here, contact the company to see if it will make the same measurements available. Or, better yet, ask if it uses the slopers from a major pattern company in order to develop their patterns, and if so, whose. When you're copying a neckline or collar, try to choose your pattern size by front neck width, selecting the closest one to your own.

Adjust the Neck Width

After pressing the commercial pattern pieces, tape those which contain the neckline onto a piece of tracing paper or gridded pattern paper. The neckline is often transformed into shapes other than oval, like on a jacket with a lapel, but it is always the seam line closest to the neck. Sometimes, part of the garment neckline is on a separate pattern piece from that which contains the CF and CB lines, like on a raglan-sleeved garment, where part of the neckline is on the sleeve pattern. In this case, you'll tape the pattern pieces together as worn, making sure that when joined, the neckline is smoothly and correctly shaped. A majority of commercial patterns have the neckline in just two pattern pieces, the front and back.

If your pattern has a neck dart (or ease) that points to the bust in front or to the shoulder blade in back, pin it out at the neckline and taper it to zero at the pivot point (the bust point in front or the approximate area of the shoulder blade in back). Then cut from the side seam to, but not through, the pivot point and let the pattern spread apart there, allowing the neckline to lay flat. NOTE: On a shawl collar, if the neck dart is double-ended (fisheye dart) and is parallel to the roll line of the jacket, disregard it; it's not a bust dart, it's a contour dart for better fit at the neck. However, many shawl collar patterns have a portion of the bust dart pivoted to the neck point so it can be hidden under the collar. This dart should be pinned out before proceeding to measure the neck width. Mark the seam lines on the center front closure, the front and back necklines, the collar, and the collar stand, where applicable. To do this, assuming the seam allowances are the standard 5/8 inch, lay a tape measure against the cutting line for the size you've selected and mark a line on the opposite side of the tape. (Make sure that the measuring tape is 5/8 inch wide; most 60 inch long ones are.) You may cut off the seam allowances if you like, after transferring any notches or match points to the inside of the seam line. Extend the center front and center back lines past the level of the neck points, and measure the fashion pattern's front and back neck width by measuring from the neck point to the extended centerline, recording the amounts in the neck area of the pattern. Compare them to the sloper's neck widths on the measurement chart to see if they've been widened. Usually, any change will be made equally on the front and back neck, but not always. Sometimes the back is widened only, by transferring part of the shoulder blade dart to the neckline and leaving it open for comfort. Sometimes the front and back are widened equally by just by moving out on the shoulder line. More rarely, part of the bust dart is moved to the front neckline and left open as ease. At any rate, any existing collar was drafted for that widened neck, so you should make the same changes on your Bodymap. (Because your Bodymap pattern was adjusted for comfort already, you may choose to widen both the back and front neckline using only the front neck width change, disregarding any *additional* widening of the back neck.) Additional back neck width will result in a slightly wider back of the garment, including a wider back neck, a collar which stands a scant bit farther away from the neck, and shoulder seam lines which may move slightly forward.

If the pattern's neck was widened, mark point "A" on the shoulder lines of your Bodymap which corresponds to the amount widened. For example, if the sloper measurement was 3, and the commercial pattern measurement was 3-1/4, the neck was widened by 1/4 inch, so mark point "A" 1/4 inch away from the neck point on your Bodymap's shoulder seam line, both on the front and back patterns.

Then, compare your personal neck widths to those of the sloper's. If there's a difference, you'll need to spread or overlap the pattern's neckline, between the centerline and the neck point. For shawl collars, cut off the back portion of the collar 1/2 inch above the neck points, parallel to the collar's CB line, and set it to the side for now. An adjustment made all the way to the CB of the collar would change the collar width, which is normally not done. You'll replace the back part of the collar after the adjustment is done, before truing. Draw a vertical line, B, that extends from the neckline to the hem line, within an inch of the centerline where possible.

Stay outside (closer to the neck points) of any collar endpoint markings on the front. This way, however, the "notched" collar points remain the same size the designer intended.

Avoid any neck dart or pleats as well, placing "B" anywhere between the CF and the neck point which doesn't intersect them (even 1/4 inch from the CF if necessary). Cut along this line and spread or overlap the pattern an amount equal to the difference between your personal neck width and the sloper's neck width. You may fold out decreases if you wish but it's more accurate to cut and overlap. In this case, if the personal measurement was 2-3/4 (front) and 3 (back), and the sloper's was 3 (front) and 3 1/8 (back), the personal neck is narrower, so you would cut and overlap B in the front by 1/4 inch, and in the back by 1/8 inch. Had the measurements been reversed, with the personal measurements wider than the sloper's, B would have been spread apart the corresponding amounts. True the seam lines on the fashion pattern with a French curve.

For drastically widened necklines, like almost-off-the-shoulder designs, you'll need the pattern company's sloper to compare another measurement, CF to Natural Shoulder Point, because these necklines are usually intended to have a certain relationship with the shoulder/arm joint, and you need to figure out what that relationship is. After adjusting the personal sloper neck widths, compare the fashion pattern's neck width to the sloper's CF to Natural Shoulder Point

Only the neck width of this commercial pattern, the "Asymmetry Tunic," from D'Leas' Fabric and Button Studio, was adjusted. Photo by Earl Gibson.

measurement. Say, for example, the sloper's measurement is 7-3/4, and the fashion pattern's is 6-3/4. This indicates that the designer intended for this neckline to be inside of the natural shoulder point 1 inch. Because your natural shoulder point is marked on your Bodymap variation pattern, make mark "A" 1 inch inside of it, towards the garment center. This is your revised neck point. Next, evaluate the neckline level as explained below before truing your pattern.

Adjust the Neck Depth

For lowered necklines that you fear may be too revealing, you need to first have an idea of the lowest point you'd be comfortable with. Say, for example, that you decide 4 inches above the bust point is the lowest acceptable level for a scoop neck. Simply mark a horizontal line at the desired neckline level, crossing CF. Place your Bodymap on top of the fashion pattern with the neckline/CF points aligned. Now trace the center portion of fashion pattern's neckline onto your Bodymap pattern, blending it to "A," your revised neck point. Check to make sure it's an acceptable neckline. Apply the contouring principles where needed as you learned in Chapters 3 and 4.

If the neckline of the fashion pattern is a jewel neck, or a high cut collar like a band (mandarin) or a turtleneck, you'll also need to compare your neck depth to the sloper's to determine if it needs to be raised, or more often, lowered. Omit this step for most other necklines, because widened and lowered necklines don't choke you. Compare your neck depth to the sloper's. To adjust, cut along line "B" to about an inch below the CF neck edge and then horizontally out on line "C" to the CF edge of the pattern. Raise or lower this small section the required amount, and true the seam lines. This should be a small adjustment—anywhere from 1/4 to 1/2 inch is average.

Do not change the roll line of a lapel to make it button higher or lower by just folding the finished garment that way, as doing so will change the width of the lower collar and the lapel. Tissue-fit the pattern to see if the depth of the opening is suitable. If not, adjust the neck depth by shortening the fashion pattern just below the neck point. Draw adjustment line "D" from about 1 inch below the neck point out to the armhole, parallel to the shoulder seam line. Spread or overlap "D" in order to change the breakpoint (the point where the buttons start) of the roll line, and adjust your collar accordingly.

True all seam lines with a French curve or straight edge as required. Add any additional tracing paper where needed to your Bodymap pattern so that you can trace the corrected markings onto it. To do this, lay the Bodymap on top of the fashion pattern, aligning the center fronts and placing the revised Bodymap neck point "A" over the fashion pattern's neck point. Trace over the revised neckline and closure.

Collars and Collar Stands

Once you've corrected the neckline, you'll most likely have to adjust the collar as well, because changes in the length of the neckline always require changes in the length of the collar. However, some neckline changes, such as when you're narrowing the width of a severely lowered neckline, do not change the length of the neckline, so you have to physically "walk" the collar around the neckline to determine whether or not it needs to be changed as well. Rarely, however is the width of the collar adjusted. (The width of a collar is the measurement of the center back line of the collar.) If the front neckline was narrowed, narrow the front neckline of the collar between the shoulder mark and the front of the collar. To do this, walk the collar around the neckline, as it will be sewn, from its match point on or near the CF till it meets vertical adjustment line "B," in order to mark the corresponding adjustment line on the collar. Do the same for the back part of the collar. Spread or overlap the collar at these lines as you did on the neckline. True your collar by walking it around the neckline, making sure all symbols match as they're supposed to. If there's a separate collar stand, adjust it first, then the collar. If you lowered the neck depth by 1/4 to 1/2 inch, it's wise to make a muslin collar and test the fit.

Special Instructions for Shaped Necklines

Shaped necklines are a bit more time consuming to trace correctly, but are easily accomplished by dividing any change among the number of shapes. Take for example, a scalloped "V" or "scoop" neckline. Neck width and depth changes as performed above would result in unequal scallops at the adjustment lines. Instead, copy the front and back scallop shapes onto a piece of tracing paper and set the tracing aside. Connect the neck points to the CF and CB at the base of the scallops. This is the actual neckline.

Measure and record the neckline length, front and back. Perform the neck width and depth changes described above, true the neckline, and measure the revised necklines. Calculate the difference on both the front and back necklines and divide the difference between the number of scallops. For example, if there are three scallops in front, and the revised front neckline is 3/4 inch less, then you'd narrow each scallop by 1/4 inch. Fold out, in this case, 1/4 inch at the center of each scallop on the copy you made, true each curve, and transfer the new scallops back onto your fashion pattern, aligning the scallop base along the revised neckline. Repeat the process on the back. Lay your Bodymap on top of the fashion pattern with neck points and center fronts matching, and trace the new scalloped neckline and closure. Sweetheart necklines are usually adjusted in the normal way, with the neck width adjustment on the horizontal, lower part of the neckline, and the neck depth adjusted like the "revealing" adjustment described earlier.

NECK WIDTH CHART:

	4	6	8	10	12	14	16	18	20	22	24
VOGUE/BUTTERICK											
front neck width	2-1/2	2-5/8	2-3/4	2-7/8	2-7/8	3	3-1/8	3-1/4	3-1/4	3-3/8	
back neck width	2-5/8	2-3/4	2-7/8	2-7/8	3	3-1/8	3-1/8	3-1/4	3-3/8	3-1/2	
BURDA											
front neck width	2-5/8	2-3/4	2-3/4	2-7/8	3	3	3	3-1/8	3-1/8		
back neck width	2-5/8	2-3/4	2-3/4	2-7/8	3	3	3	3-1/8	3-1/8		
SIMPLICITY											
front neck width	2-1/4	2-3/8	2-1/2	2-5/8	2-3/4	2-7/8	3	3-1/8	3-3/8	3-1/2	3-5/8
back neck width	2-1/2	2-5/8	2-3/4	2-7/8	3	3-1/8	3-1/4	3-3/8	3-1/2	3-5/8	3-3/4
STYLE											
front neck width	2-5/8	2-5/8	2-3/4	2-7/8	3	3-1/8					
back neck width	3	3	3-1/8	3-3/8	3-3/8	3-1/2					
MCCALLS											
front neck width	2-5/8	2-5/8	2-5/8	2-3/4	2-3/4	2-7/8	2-7/8	3	3-1/8		
back neck width	2-3/4	2-3/4	2-3/4	3	3	3-1/8	3-1/8	3-1/4	3-3/8		

INDEX

A

Arm fullness 13
Armhole 7, 12-14, 19, 21, 24, 26, 28-30, 39, 42-43, 47, 49, 51-62, 65-70, 72-73, 79-83, 85-86, 88-95, 97-98, 101, 113-114, 118
Armhole width 39, 47, 52-53
Asymmetrical 9, 24, 114-115

B

Back neck 10, 12, 19, 22-23, 34-35, 41, 48, 50, 52, 117, 119
Balanced 7
Base pattern 7, 9, 15, 31, 39, 55, 63-65, 68, 70-75, 77, 80, 82-84, 90, 94, 96, 116
Bias grain line 8-9, 103
Bicep line 12, 33-34, 60-62, 108-110
Bicep width 13
Bodymap 7, 9, 12, 15, 18-19, 23, 31, 33-34, 36, 38-40, 43-44, 49-52, 55, 59-60, 62, 66, 114, 116, 118-119
Bodymap Variation Patterns 116, 118
Bodymapping 7-9, 12-13, 15, 17-19, 21, 23, 25, 36, 64, 66, 116
Broad or narrow shoulders 7
Bust 6-7, 9-12, 14, 18-19, 24, 26, 30, 32, 35-36, 42-43, 53, 59, 66, 70, 72, 78, 80, 82, 99, 114-115, 117
Bust dart angle 9-10, 35, 39, 47, 49, 83, 114-115
Bust line 11, 107, 112
Bust points 7, 19, 29, 31, 36, 43-44, 115-116
Bust shaping 10, 66, 72, 83, 89

C

Cap height 13, 19, 34-35, 60-61, 108
Center back (CB) 12, 14, 19, 21, 23-24, 28-30, 37, 41, 49-52, 54-55, 57-58, 67, 72, 81, 85, 98, 100-101, 103-107, 112-113, 116-119
Center back (CB) neck point 10, 19, 22, 39, 41, 49, 58, 72, 105
Closure 112, 117, 119
Collar(s) 65-66, 101-107, 116-119
Commercial sewing patterns 6-7, 15, 66
Cross grain line 6-9, 13-14, 18-19, 21, 23-25, 28-31, 40, 59

Crosswise grain line 8, 19, 28, 30
Cup size 6, 10-11

D

Dart 7-10, 13-15, 18, 28, 31, 36-37, 39, 42-43, 45-47, 51, 53, 56-58, 65-69, 71-75, 77-78, 80-83, 85, 91, 93, 95, 97-98, 105, 114-115, 117
Dart legs 9, 45-47, 52, 56, 59, 70, 74-75, 78
Diagonal folds 12-14, 24, 26, 29, 72, 114
Dowager's hump 10, 28, 52, 57, 59

E

Ease 6-7, 9, 13, 47, 58-59, 66-68, 72, 78, 80, 82, 86, 110, 117
Equalized armhole 64, 72-73, 86, 88-89, 91-92

F

Facing 68, 113
Figure flaws 14
Fitting 6-10, 12-13, 15, 24, 28, 40-41, 43, 53, 57, 66-67, 70-71, 83, 95, 100
Fitting by grain 7-9
Fitting shell 6-7, 9, 15, 117
French curve 7, 14, 21, 37-38, 46-47, 49, 52, 54-55, 59, 61, 78, 80, 91, 104, 111, 118

G

Gathers 9
Grading 11
Grain up 8, 18
Grain-controlling darts 10, 66

H

High or shallow neck base 7
Horizontal 6-9, 11-12, 22, 24-26, 28-30, 36-37, 46, 49, 51, 60-61, 72, 99, 103, 118-119

J

Jewel 14, 68, 103, 116, 118

K

Kimono 65, 67, 69, 72, 86-88, 93
Knit(s) 8, 18, 65, 70, 102

L

Large or thin neck 7
Lengthwise grain line 8, 30
Lowered shoulder 9-10, 114

M

Manipulated 9, 18, 65, 68, 74

N

Neck depth 118-119
Neck points 9-12, 19, 21, 24, 34, 41-42, 49-50, 52, 56, 72-73, 90-91, 98, 117-119
Neck size 7, 11, 20-21
Neck width 11, 19-20, 35, 39-40, 52, 117-119
Necklines 65, 68, 90, 102-103, 113, 116-119

O

Off-grain 8, 18, 28, 31, 40, 43
On-grain 8, 18-19

P

Panel style line 65, 82-83
Parallel 7, 9, 11-12, 19-20, 23-25, 28, 33-34, 36, 44, 46, 50-52, 54, 57, 72, 84, 86, 98, 107, 109, 112, 117-118
Pattern alteration 6, 9
Pattern making 7, 65-66, 113-114
Pivot point 9, 117
Pivoting 9, 73
Pleats 9, 37, 65, 108, 111, 118
Pockets 69
Posture 6, 7, 11-12, 24, 53, 61
Princess line 12, 15, 25, 59, 65, 73, 76-81, 88, 92, 113, 116
Proper balance 11
Proportion 6, 11
Protruding abdomen 12, 25, 28, 32, 39-40, 43, 45-46, 56, 58
Protruding buttocks 12, 39-40, 50, 56, 58

R

Raglan 65, 72, 88-92, 116-117

S

Seam lines 7, 36, 38-39, 41-42, 52, 55, 62, 68, 72-73, 78, 80, 82, 102, 117-118
Selvage 8, 18, 119
Set-in sleeve(s) 12, 15, 34, 60, 66, 69
Shaping 9-10, 14-15, 18, 36, 65-67, 72, 74-75, 83, 89
Shoulder blade(s) 6, 10-12, 14, 19, 26, 28-29, 32, 39, 42, 51-52, 57, 115, 117
Shoulder pad height 60, 114
Shoulder point(s) 10, 13, 22, 24, 33-34, 47, 55, 57, 60, 70, 72-73, 81, 86-88, 91, 93-94, 97-99, 101-104, 114, 116, 118
Shoulder seam 9, 11-14, 19, 33-35, 39, 41-42, 49-53, 55-57, 60-61, 69, 71-72, 75, 77-78, 84, 86, 91, 95, 98, 105, 108, 114, 116-118
Shoulder slope dart 10, 19, 23, 31-32, 36, 39, 49, 114-115
Slashing 9
Sleeve cap 12-13, 60, 91, 93, 108, 110
Sloper 6-7, 9, 64, 66, 116-118
Spreading 9, 15, 59, 73, 85
Square or sloped shoulders 7, 55
Standard grading chart 11
Standard measurements 11
Straight back 28
Straight grain line 8
Straight of grain 8, 107

T

Tailored sleeve 12
Take-up 8-10, 31, 36, 39, 45, 57, 67, 111
True 7-8, 14, 37-39, 52, 54-55, 58-59, 68, 72, 74, 80, 84, 86-87, 94, 98, 104, 106, 110
True bias 8, 14
Tucks 37

U

Underarm level 12-13, 19, 28, 30, 33, 39, 43-44, 47, 49, 51-53, 57, 60, 78, 114
Underarm point 12, 39, 49, 51-54, 56, 58, 60-63, 66, 70-73, 82, 86, 90, 92, 94-95, 97-100, 114, 116
Underlay 8, 37, 73-75, 85
Upper back dart angles 35, 39, 42, 114
Upper back darts 10, 13, 19, 26, 29, 36, 39, 40, 52-53, 56-57, 59-60, 72, 78, 81, 85, 89-90, 95, 98, 115

V

Vertical 8, 12, 19, 24-25, 29-30, 36-38, 44, 46, 50-52, 66, 73, 82, 118-119

W

Waist dart(s) 10, 12, 14, 19, 29, 31-32, 36, 39, 43-46, 51, 58, 66-67, 70, 77-78, 80-83, 88
Waist shaping 10, 14, 18, 66, 83
Waistline 7, 18, 32, 39, 43-44, 51, 61, 70, 77, 99, 107, 112
Waistline seam 6-7, 12, 14, 24-25, 28
Warp threads 8
Weft threads 8

Y

Yoke 64, 84-85, 113